GOD, MEDICINE, AND SUFFERING

God,
Medicine, and
Suffering

Stanley Hauerwas

WILLIAM B. EERDMANS PUBLISHING COMPANY
GRAND RAPIDS, MICHIGAN

Printed in the United States of America

First published 1990 as
Naming the Silences: God, Medicine, and the Problem of Suffering

Reprinted with new title 1994

Library of Congress Cataloging-in-Publication Data

Hauerwas, Stanley, 1940 –
    God, medicine, and suffering / Stanley Hauerwas.
        p.   cm.
    Includes index.
    ISBN 0–8028–0896–4
    1. Suffering — Religious aspects — Christianity.
    2. Children — Death — Religious aspects — Christianity.
    3. Theodicy. 4. Medicine — Religious aspects — Christianity.
    5. Christianity — 20th century. 6. Consolation. 7. Christian
    ethics — Methodist authors. I. Title.
    BT732.7.H38   1990
    231′.8 — dc20
                                                        90–44121
                                                        CIP

The author and publisher gratefully acknowledge permission granted
by the publishers listed on page 152 to use extended quotations from
copyrighted works.

To
Kelli and Logan
For their courage, compassion, and grace
and to
Sarah Austin
who is the joy

I have been daily grateful for the friend who remarked that grief isolates. He did not mean only that I, grieving, am isolated from you, happy. He meant also that *shared* grief isolates the sharers from each other. Though united in that we are grieving, we grieve differently. As each death has its own character, so too each grief over a death has its own character—its own escape. The dynamics of each person's sorrow must be allowed to work themselves out without judgment. I may find it strange that you should be tearful today but dry-eyed yesterday when my tears were yesterday. But my sorrow is not your sorrow.

There's something more: I must struggle so hard to regain life that I cannot reach out to you. Nor you to me. The one not grieving must touch us both. It's when people are happy that they say, "Let's get together."

(Nicholas Wolterstorff, *Lament for a Son*)

Contents

Preface

I should like to write a book to help people cope with inexplicable pain and suffering—a book like Harold Kushner's *When Bad Things Happen to Good People*. To write such a book one would have to be a poet, since only the poets, poets like the Psalmist, know how to touch our souls with words so that we may be comforted. I am not a poet, but only a theologian. So even though this is a book about theodicy, illness, and medicine, I cannot pretend that it can help those who have had a spouse die unexpectedly, who have experienced the death of a child, or who have gone through some equally troubling event.

In this book I make no attempt to explain such evil or to explain why a good and all-powerful God allows us to undergo suffering for seemingly no reason. For a number of reasons that I hope this book will make clear, I am profoundly suspicious of all attempts such as Kushner's to explain why God allows us to experience pain and suffering; put even more strongly, I hope to show why this way of putting the question of suffering is a theological mistake. Even if I were able to supply such an "explanation," I suspect it would do little to comfort a couple whose child has just been diagnosed as having incurable cancer. Rather than trying to answer the question of why God allows evil and suffering, I will try to help us understand why that question seems so important to us who inhabit the world we call modern and why illness seems so often to occasion such questions.

It would be foolhardy, however, to deny the desire many feel to seek an explanation for suffering and pain. Even if I am able to show that such explanations are theologically and philosophically wrongheaded, the fact remains that when most of us are confronted with the illness or death of our child or a friend's child, we want an explanation. It is almost as if we have a primitive need to know that such an illness or death does not render our existence and God's existence absurd. I will try to show that this seemingly "primitive need" has a particular form today that is often based on destructive presuppositions about the nature of our existence. Moreover, if we are to rightly express our care for one another through the office of medicine, it is imperative that we understand those presuppositions and why they have such a hold on us.

So, although this book has to do with theodicy and medicine, it focuses primarily on why the problem of illness and death—particularly the problem of childhood illness and death—is so troubling for us. I am not trying to write a book that rivals Rabbi Kushner's; rather, I am attempting to understand why his book has struck a chord in so many people. Kushner has given voice to a question asked by many: "Why do bad things happen to good people?" The interesting issue is not whether he has rightly or wrongly answered that question, but rather why that question is being asked now and primarily about children we cannot, despite the sophistication of our medical care, save from suffering and death.

By exploring this question I hope to help some people by enabling them to name the powers that possess us. No powers determine our lives more completely than those we think we have under our control. I believe that the most decisive challenge which the experience of childhood illness presents is our inability to name the silences such illness creates. Modern medicine can and too often has become a noisy way to hide those silences. I will try to show how the God whom Christians worship can give a voice to that pain in a manner that at least gives us a way to go on.

Even though this is a book about theodicy, I spend little time exploring the logical and philosophical issues usually associated with discussions of theodicy. Rather, I begin with a discussion of childhood illness and our attempt to care for ill children through medicine. I have concentrated on the problem of ill children because they seem to present us with the hardest case. For some reason, adult illness does not disturb us in the same way. Why the illness of children bothers us so deeply and in particular why it challenges our understanding of God are finally what this book is about— though in Chapter Three I will try to delineate the continuities and the discontinuities between a child's death and and an adult's death.

My attempt to understand why these matters are related has compelled me to discuss questions about the nature and kinds of suffering, the role and nature of medicine in our lives, and finally our understanding of God. I cannot promise readers consolation, but only as honest an account as I can give of why we cannot afford to give ourselves explanations for evil when what is required is a community capable of absorbing our grief.

Although there is a rationale for the way I've organized the chapters of this book, I do not pretend that readers will find a clear line of argument from one chapter to the next. Chapters Two and Three are basically commentaries on the story I tell in Chapter One. In Chapter Two I argue on theological grounds against the very idea of theodicy as a theoretical enterprise. In Chapter Three I go over some of the same ground but concentrate on how medicine as an activity of service becomes distorted when we try to use it to eliminate the silence created by death.

Much of this book is made up of stories about ill and dying children. Thus the first chapter is an examination of *The Blood of the Lamb,* Peter DeVries's haunting novel about a father's relationship with his daughter, who is dying of leukemia; the second chapter ends with a look at *Where Is God When a Child Suffers?*, Penny Giesbrecht's account of her struggle to care for her son, Jeremy, who was diagnosed as "autistic-like"; and the final chapter concludes with an extended discussion of two books: *The Private Worlds of Dying Children,* Myra Bluebond-Langner's observations about children dying of leukemia, and Nicholas Wolterstorff's *Lament for a Son,* the diary of a grieving father whose son was killed in a mountain-climbing accident. That this book is primarily made up of these stories is its basic "argument." The reader will find no theoretical discussion of the nature of narrative qua narrative here, because I am increasingly convinced that such analysis does little to help us understand the story of God. I am convinced, however, that it is only as we are able to locate our lives in relation to those lives which manifest God's glory that we are graced with the resources necessary to live with our silences.

Throughout this book I appeal to a "we" to indicate my intended audience. By that "we" I mean people who worship God by the name of Father, Son, and Holy Spirit. I assume that such worshipers, like me, lead lives which are often at odds with the One who compels our devotion. Accordingly, I write for Christians in the hope that theological reflection might give them some help in living more faithful lives. I also hope, however, that this book might be of some help to non-Christians—that at the very least it might help them to recognize the significance of the absence of such worship.

While I was writing this book, many people helped me by sharing their time and their lives. I am particularly grateful to Reinhard Hutter for reading and criticizing the manuscript. My colleague, Professor Ken Surin, has made invaluable contributions to my consideration of these issues—not only through the conversations we have had but also through his own book, *Theology and the Problem of Evil*. Professors Jefferson Powell and Greg Jones also read an earlier version of the manuscript and made invaluable suggestions. Mr. Phil Kenneson has endured going over these matters with me during our runs together and has also offered incisive comments on the manuscript itself. I have learned much from his trenchant criticism. I am also indebted to Dr. Earl Shelp, who suggested I write the book. Dr. Robert Nelson, Director of the Institute of Religion, was my gracious host when I delivered the Forem Lecture at the institute, the seed from which this book grew. I am indebted both to him and to the institute for their support of this project. Delivering the Pastoral Lectures at the University of Durham in 1989 gave me an opportunity to see how others would respond to the themes of this book. I am indebted to the wonderful reception and comments I received there; I learned much from them. Professor Dan Hardy and Mrs. Perrin Hardy were wonderful hosts to me, a stranger in their midst. As usual, Mrs. Gay Trotter typed and retyped the manuscript with the efficiency and good spirit that is her wonderful gift to combine in one life.

While I was writing this book, I became seriously ill for the first time in my life. Adam, my son, and Paula, now my wife, saw me through my illness, and in the process they taught me much about how to receive care. I am one of the fortunate ones, for whatever small suffering I have had in my life, that suffering has always been bounded by greater gifts. The happiness that Paula has given me is a joy I had not imagined. It is odd, but I think true, that most of us are almost as ill-prepared to receive joy as we are suffering.

CHAPTER I

A Child's Dying

On Getting the Issues Right: A Story

It is one thing to think that "the problem of evil" can be answered by the "free-will" defense or explained through human sin; it is quite another to confront the illness of a child. This is as true for the most convinced believer as it is for the half-convinced or the convinced unbeliever. It is speculatively interesting to ask how the existence of a good and all-powerful God can be reconciled with the existence of evil in the world; how we answer that question may even be the way we justify our belief—or explain our unbelief. But when I confront the actual suffering and threatened death of a child—in particular, the actual suffering and threatened death of my child—such speculative considerations grounding belief or unbelief seem hollow.

That is the way it should be. One of the difficulties with books about "the problem of evil" is that they seldom raise the question of who has the right to ask the question and from what set of presuppositions. Sitting in my office reflecting on the problem of evil is more like a game than a serious activity. I'm not even sure that I have the right to engage in such speculation, since little about the way I live my life hinges on the answer, no matter what it may turn out to be. The question "Why does evil exist?" is asked as if it makes sense from anyone's perspective. But we are not "anyone"; we are people who exist at this point in time, with this particular set of convictions, in relation to these friends and this community, and who have these particular hopes and desires. Only within such a context does the question of suffering become serious. We are, quite rightly, not interested in the theoretical issue of suffering and evil; rather, we are torn apart by what is happening to real people, to those we know and love.

That is why I begin with a story. We shall see that such stories are much more than illustrations of the problem of evil. Indeed, without such stories we would have no means to frame the challenge of suffering, and even more important, no way to respond to that challenge. The kinds of suffering that drive us mad are those that we say have no point. But it isn't always clear what we mean when we talk about pointless suffering. Ostensibly we usually means suffering that as far as we can see has no good results. Yet "results" too often are strained and offer too-easy comfort. By "no point" I think what we really mean is that we cannot situate this life with its suffering in any ongoing story carried by a community that can make this suffering person's life its own. So I begin by telling a story.

The story I am going to tell is labeled "fiction," but that doesn't mean that it's not a true story. Rather, "fiction" simply names the fact that the story is in the form of a novel by Peter DeVries called *The Blood of the Lamb*.[1] In fact, the novel is based on a tragedy that DeVries himself experienced. That might partly explain why this novel is so uncharacteristic of DeVries. Usually he writes wonderfully witty, satirical novels filled with the muddles that we humans create for ourselves through our penchant for being forever dissatisfied with our lot. Although *The Blood of the Lamb* contains wit, and its main character, Don Wanderhope, approaches life with DeVries's own wry skepticism, it has a seriousness which suggests "this happened." But in the end the fact that something very much like this happened to DeVries is of no matter. What is important is that this story has the ring of truth which comes only through concreteness.

Tolstoy observed that all happy marriages are similar, but all unhappy marriages are different. There seems something right about this observation, though it is by no means easy to say why. I suspect the difference between happiness and suffering is that the latter creates a silence which is not easily shared. No two sufferings are the same: my suffering, for example, occurs in the context of my personal history and thus is peculiarly mine. Few of us have the gift to tell the story of our suffering in a manner that enables us to share it with others. The gift as well as the burden of the artist is to be able to tell the story so that others may have some idea of what his or her suffering is like.

---

1. Peter DeVries, *The Blood of the Lamb* (Boston: Little, Brown & Co., 1969). All subsequent references to the novel will appear parenthetically in the text. For a wonderful analysis of DeVries's work, and in particular *The Blood of the Lamb*, see Ralph Wood's essay entitled "The Comedy of Unconditional Election and Irresistible Grace," in his *Comedy of Redemption: Christian Faith and Comic Vision in Four American Novelists* (Notre Dame: University of Notre Dame Press, 1988), pp. 252-79.

The Blood of the Lamb is a novel about the dying and death of Don Wanderhope's daughter, Carol, who succumbs to leukemia at the age of eleven. The main character of the novel, however, is Don. In fact, Carol's dying is the focal point of only the last third of the book; roughly two-thirds of the book is about Don Wanderhope's life and doubts. Don's last name says quite a bit about him. He is the son of a Dutch immigrant who had come to America intending only to visit some friends and relatives. However, on his way across the Atlantic Don's father had become so seasick that he couldn't face the prospect of a return voyage. Rather than return, he did the next best thing—he lived out his life in Chicago. Such are the contingencies that make up our lives.

Although Ben Wanderhope, Don's father, may have been something less than a "fearless voyager" of the sea, he certainly is such from an intellectual perspective. Schooled in the Bible in the way only a Dutch Calvinist could have been, Ben never tires of raising troubling issues about his religious beliefs. This explains the kind of conversations he has with Don's uncle, a Dutch Calvinist minister named Hans:

> "How about me?" my father said. . . . "How about me in doubt and turmoil? That's all well and good, Hans, but what I'm trying to say is, one error in the Bible and the doctrine of infallibility goes to pieces. It's all or nothing."
>
> "Then take it all, Ben," my uncle said. "We must put away the pride of the flesh, of which the reason is a part, and accept salvation as we accept a mystery. For he who finds himself shall lose himself, and he who loses himself shall find himself. Like I said Sunday."
>
> "And the virgin birth. We get that in a chapter where the lineage is traced through Joseph. How can those two things be true?" (p. 6)

This restlessness of spirit affects both of Ben's sons—
Louie, the older boy, who loses his faith during his medical
studies at the University of Chicago, and Don, who thinks
that Louie can do no wrong. But in the home of a Dutch
Calvinist there is no such thing as atheism in general. The
God who is disbelieved is the God who alone could save
humankind from total depravity. It is this God that Don
soon engages in struggle when Louie, the beloved brother,
the brother of such great promise and style, dies of pneumonia:

> My sensation, rather than fear or piety, was a baffled and
> uncomprehending rage. That flesh with which I had lain in
> comradely embrace destroyable, on such short notice, by a
> whim known as divine? . . . Who wantonly scattered such
> charm, who broke such flesh like bread for his purposes? In
> later years, years which brought me to another such vigil
> over one more surely my flesh and blood, I came to under-
> stand a few things about what people believe. What people
> believe is a measure of what they suffer. "The Lord giveth
> and the Lord taketh away"—there must be balm of some
> sort in that for men whose treasures have been confiscated.
> These displaced Dutch fisherfolk, these farmers peddling
> coal and ice in a strange land, must have had their reasons
> for worshiping a god scarcely distinguishable from the devil
> they feared. But the boy kneeling on the parlor floor was
> shut off from such speculatory solaces. All the theologies
> inherent in the minister's winding drone came down to this:
> Believe in God and don't put anything past him. Or another
> thought formed itself in the language of the streets in which
> the boy had learned crude justice and mercy: *"Why doesn't
> He pick on somebody his size?"* (pp. 24-25)

Of course Don's life goes on, and he, like his father,
fluctuates wildly between Faith and Reason. But in his

younger years these issues of belief and unbelief take a back seat to what at the time are more important concerns for Don, such as exploring the wonders of sex and finding out if he can climb a few rungs of the social ladder. Although Don is desperate to engage in both these activities, he is not overly successful in either. His search for sexual fulfillment starts promisingly with a young Italian Catholic woman named Maria, whose "warm and spontaneous nature" makes her rather open in matters of sex. Unfortunately, however, the long built-up climax of this relationship is interrupted by O'Malley, the cop who is patrolling the park and discovers the couple at the wrong time.

Don's climb up the social ladder gets off to a more promising start with his enrollment in the University of Chicago. To help pay for this expensive undertaking, Don continues to help his father with his sanitation business, although he is constantly afraid that he will be spotted at this task near the university. As he picks up the garbage of the upper middle class, he longs to gain entry to the elegant homes of the elegant people who inhabit them; they seem to represent all he desires. He does succeed in gaining entry through Archie Winkler, who brings Don home one afternoon after Don offers Archie "some whispered aid" during a biology quiz. But this relationship doesn't turn out to be the boon Don anticipates it will be. Although Archie's family is rich and socially prominent, Archie soon owes Don almost two hundred dollars, and he refuses to pay it back even after Don's family falls on hard times when his father develops strange neurological symptoms. Desperate, Don attempts to retrieve the money he's owed from Archie's room when he goes to a party at the Winklers' home, but he gets caught in the act. Thus ends his chance to be part of the Eden of the American upper class.

Although what Don calls his "first assault on the strongholds of fashion" (p. 66) fails, the possibility of sexual conquest begins to look more promising when Greta Wigbaldy appears on the scene. Both she and Don are detached enough from their Dutch Reformed background to begin to move away from the City of God. Tired of making out in the most uncomfortable of places, Greta suggests they go to one of the model homes built by her father, a building contractor busy constructing his version of the American dream. But the very first night that Don and Greta slip away for a forbidden hour together is the night that Mr. and Mrs. Wigbaldy show this occupied "dream house" to a prospective buyer. Being caught in the act, however, helps Don discover that he shares with Greta more than just the physical—not only hatred of the prosaic little houses her father has built (one of which Mr. Wigbaldy promises the couple as an inducement to marriage) but, even more, the dread of marriage itself.

Before matters with Greta can progress, however, Don is diagnosed (probably mistakenly) as having tuberculosis by Doc Berkenbosch, who had gone to "one of the worst medical schools in the country at a time when medical schools were a scandal" (p. 17). Since he is the family doctor, there is no question that his advice to send Don to the church sanitarium in Colorado must be followed. This has two results: it ends the Wigbaldys' plans for Don and Greta's marriage, and it also insures Ben Wanderhope's return to the church. Ben has been close to excommunication since experiencing "a renaissance of his Doubt stimulated by a reading of the atheistic pamphlets of Robert Ingersoll" (p. 79). But then he discovers that the sanitarium will cost triple the normal price if he is not in good standing with the church; as his brother Jake exclaims, "You see what you get for doubting God's word? Terrible expense!" (p. 80). In the face of this threat, he experiences "a sudden and radical change of heart" (p. 79).

So Don Wanderhope begins his pilgrimage in sickness, but discovers that the Dutch Reformed sanitarium is not the retreat he has imagined it would be. When Dr. Simpson examines him, Don discovers that he has a very slight case, if any, of TB, and that the cure will depend largely on his attitude. Dr. Simpson observes,

> "I used to think mental attitude half the battle, then seventy-five per cent of the cure; now I'm not sure it isn't more like ninety-five. Or maybe I should say ninety-eight six." The ironic grin conveyed the malicious implication not to be stated: that if one determined the prolongation of a disease, mightn't one also have willed its acquisition? "I have more people in here than I can tell you, about whom I wonder what they're running away from. You will no doubt make a game of picking them out for yourself." (p. 87)

After a series of encounters with other "lungers," Don begins to wonder if there isn't a better way of evading reality. But then he meets Rena Baker, a pony-tailed blonde who is very religious and very sick. Soon she is confined to bed, which gives her and Don, who has fallen in love with her, opportunities for extended conversation. One of their conversations is particularly revealing:

> "Are you an atheist?"
> "Not a very devout one," I reassured her, smiling from my chair. "I'm backsliding fast."
> "Do you believe in a God?"
> "With nothing certain, anything is possible."
> "You're slippery as an eel, aren't you? Do you believe you have a soul?"

"No, but I believe you do." . . .

"Do you pray for me?"

"Well, that would mean the one I was addressing had done this to you to begin with, which I find hard to believe anybody would."

"I don't quite follow you."

"I simply mean that asking Him to cure you—or me, or anybody—implies a personal being who arbitrarily does us this dirt. The prayer then is a plea to have a heart. To knock it off. I find the thought repulsive. I prefer to think we're victims of chance to dignifying any such force with the name of Providence."

"We're supposed to deserve it." . . .

"Not you."

"I'm a sinner."

"Stop giving yourself airs. . . ."

"What would you do if you were God?"

"Put a stop to all this theology." . . .

"If we could only kiss," she said, pressing my fingers to her cheek. (pp. 103-4)

Don and Rena do finally make love as best they can, but soon afterward Don finds Rena's room empty. She had been taken to surgery to have ribs removed—"the last resort for patients whom . . . other measures had failed" (p. 106). She dies, which is a wrenching experience for Don—first Louie, now Rena. But when he talks with Dr. Simpson, he realizes that he's not the only one who has experienced suffering and loss:

"It may be a mercy, because frankly she didn't stand a chance. I doubt whether the collapse [of the lung] would have helped. It might have been a nasty third act."

"I admire the objectivity of science," I said, pacing helplessly about the room. "How they can—I had a brother once . . . Surely you no longer think this is a managed universe?"

"Why do you think you have anything to tell me, young man? I had a son once, whom I had to watch die of leukemia. He was seven. Stevie. He was such a boy as you see riding dolphins in the fountains in the parks. A dolphin boy. A faun. I watched him bleed to death."

"What did you do then, sing 'Come Thou fount of every blessing, tune my heart to sing Thy praise'?"

"Go on. I am an old man. I have shed my tears. Go ahead." . . . After an audible swallow of brandy [he] grunted apologetically and said, "Death is the commonest thing in the universe. What was this girl to you?"

"I was in love with her." . . .

"Did you kiss her?"

"Of course."

"You may live to regret it. Or then again, you may not," he added with one of his grim little jokes.

I set my brandy down and said: "Dr. Simpson, do you believe in a God?"

He just perceptibly raised his eyes, as if in entreaty to Heaven to spare him at least this. It took me some years to attain his mood and understand my blunder. He resented such questions as people do who have thought a great deal about them. The superficial and the slipshod have ready answers, but those looking this complex life straight in the eye acquire a wealth of perception so composed of delicately balanced contradictions that they dread, or resent, the call to couch any part of it in a bland generalization. The vanity (if not outrage) of trying to cage this dance of atoms in a single definition may give the weariness of age with the cry of youth for answers the appearance of boredom. Dr. Simpson looked bored as he ground his teeth and gazed away.

"Oh, one man's opinion about these things is as good as another's," he said. "You believe what you must in order to stave off the conviction that it's all a tale told by an idiot. You know, of course, you took a chance with that girl."

"It was worth it," I retorted, bitterly. (pp. 109-11)

Don has little time to mourn Rena, for it is not long after her death that he begins to receive letters from home indicating that his father is going out of his mind: "Once she [Don's mother] found him in the kitchen at three o'clock in the morning swatting cockroaches with her brassière. To the aforementioned, add what was happening on the route. There he had taken to picking up garbage from one stop and leaving it at another" (p. 113). Don is acidly philosophical about this: "The world, as has been noted, is full of a number of things, and while they may not suffice to keep us happy as kings, the troubles in which they mainly abound are diverse enough for one to distract us from the other" (p. 112). In response to the situation at home, Don leaves the sanitarium to take care of his father. After placing his father in a nursing home, Don again takes up his life, noting, "There seems to be little support in reality for the popular belief that we are mellowed by suffering. Happiness mellows us, not troubles; pleasure, perhaps, even more than happiness" (p. 120).

Yet life does hold some unexpected surprises for Don. One Sunday while visiting his father, Don encounters Greta in the same institution; she is thin and listless. According to Mrs. Wigbaldy, Greta never recovered from the experience in the model home. Feeling some obligation, Don begins to visit Greta every weekend, and she soon begins to improve. Finally Don asks her to marry him, and Greta agrees, but just before the marriage she confesses to Don that it wasn't the experience with him that caused her depression but a later one with a married man which resulted in a pregnancy and a child given up for adoption. Don is angry at first, feeling used, but in the end he decides not to renege on his proposal: "After all we've been through? The world is too many for me, baby. God knows I can't make head or tail of it alone. I doubt whether two people can either, but I guess there's no harm in their trying" (p. 134).

After Don and Greta marry, Don sells the garbage disposal route and returns to school—not to the University of Chicago but to a downtown school with a good business administration department. After graduating, he goes into advertising. His next difficulty develops midway through his second year of marriage, when Greta experiences a conversion after she begins attending a different church that is "revivalistic in nature." Unable to become pregnant, she becomes obsessed with her past indiscretion—the affair and the child she gave up—and seeks Don's condemnation of it. Because Don refuses to call her past actions a sin, he becomes the object of Greta's scorn as well as that of the "Tabernacle evangelist to whom she had confessed her guilt" (p. 138), Reverend Tonkle, who finds Don's attitude toward Greta's past to be nothing less than immoral. The gulf between Don and Greta grows wider when Don refuses to attend Reverend Tonkle's "Tabernacle" after an exploratory visit or two. But these troubles vanish as suddenly as they appeared when Greta unexpectedly becomes pregnant. This bliss is short-lived, however. When Don blunders into recounting to Greta his brother Louie's argument with Uncle Hans about how "the stages of evolution are enacted in the human embryo" (p. 141), this triggers another crisis of faith for Greta, and Reverend Tonkle reappears on the scene. Although Don aggressively brings this episode to a close, Greta's instability continues.

Time goes by, and soon Don has been transferred to a

A Child's Dying

company in the East, finds himself prospering "within the
modest range possible in that firm" (p. 143), and has a
three-year-old daughter, Carol. He and Greta have made the
customary move to Westchester and have acquired a maid,
Mrs. Brodhag, whose virtues, long formed by Congre-
gational practice, keep the family going. This is important,
because Greta continues to decline: she begins to drink
heavily and has an affair. When Don finds out about the
other man, he is enraged, but he realizes in retrospect that
he was dealing with something larger than unfaithfulness:
"Her conduct, and especially the shrill manner in which she
defended it, should have reminded me that I was dealing
with instability rather than infidelity" (p. 146). This insight
is confirmed when, after one unsuccessful attempt, Greta
ends her troubled life.

But grace has entered Don Wanderhope's life in Carol.
He is captivated by her toddler's habit of saying "Hi" every
time she sees him in the house. He is beguiled by her when,
at her fourth birthday party, she asks another child who
appears to be getting ill, "If you're going to be sick, may I
have your orange slices?" (p. 150). He loves her loving an
old dog that she defends as "part pedigree." Wanderhope
admits that he can't imagine life without her: "What, I
thought to myself as I gazed at Carol, if anything should
happen to that creature" (p. 150), this child who was so full
of grace that "you could hold her on your outstretched palm
and she would balance perfectly" (p. 151). After Greta's
death, Wanderhope and Carol, with Mrs. Brodhag in tow,
move further out to the country, where they enter into the
wonderful world of a little girl's growing up.

Carol's religious education is given over to Mrs. Brodhag, who takes her to the nearby Congregationalist Sunday
school for a year. "Coaxed" into church on Christmas after-

noon to see Carol take part in a candlelight service, Wanderhope is reminded of his worship among the Reformed:

> Memories of flowerless services and grim interrogations in
> catechism class, of Sunday afternoons at home wreathed with
> the smells of coffee and of cigars brandished by uncles locked
> in eternal dispute, of Old World women, their fat knuckles
> wound in handkerchiefs soaked in cologne, listening respect-
> fully while their menfolk gave each other chapter and verse,
> all returned to me now. These memories were like flowers
> themselves, long hidden in corners of my heart, made sud-
> denly to unfold their petals and yield their essences in a
> white New England meetinghouse so far in space and spirit
> from the church in whose shadow I had lived my boyhood.
> "Too bad you don't have more feeling for those things," Mrs.
> Brodhag would again say! And I twisting in my pew while
> every known emotion blazed within me. I thanked God
> when, propelled by a last, deranging squall of organ music
> into the winter twilight, I felt the cold air on my cheeks
> and my daughter's warm hand in mine. (p. 157)

Although Wanderhope misses his wife, he takes great
pleasure in his life with Carol. He realizes just how bucolic
this life has been when Carol, now eleven, becomes ill. She
develops a persistent temperature that antibiotics cannot
eliminate, and she has recurrent back pain. Because of the
back pain, Dr. Cameron hospitalizes her for testing. Wanderhope fears what the results might be: "My heart sank at the
specters that raised their heads. Rheumatic fever, crippling
arthritis. . . . This was a dream of a child. Hair like cornsilk,
blue bird's-wings eyes, and a carriage that completed the
resemblance to a fairy sprite. One would not have been
surprised to see her take off and fly away in a glimmer of
unsuspected wings" (p. 165). The first diagnosis is decep-

tively simple: Carol has strep throat. She improves rapidly, and Dr. Cameron offers Wanderhope an optimistic prognosis: "She feels a lot better. Give it another day and you can take her home. But anyhow, we've eliminated everything serious" (pp. 165-66). Wanderhope remembers his euphoric response:

> *That* was the happiest moment of my life. Or the next several days were the happiest days of my life. The fairy would not become a gnome. We could break bread in peace again, my child and I. The greatest experience open to man then is the recovery of the commonplace. Coffee in the morning and whiskeys in the evening again without fear. Books to read without that shadow falling across the page. Carol curled up with one in her chair and I in mine. . . . You can multiply for yourself the list of pleasures to be extorted from Simple Things when the world has once again been restored to you. (p. 166)

Buoyed by this return to the normal, Wanderhope throws himself into neglected correspondence, part of which includes a request from the editors of his college newspaper for a brief statement (two hundred words or less) of his philosophy of life. In response he writes,

> "I believe that man must learn to live without those consolations called religious, which his own intelligence must by now have told him belong to the childhood of the race. Philosophy can really give us nothing permanent to believe either; it is too rich in answers, each canceling out the rest. The quest for Meaning is foredoomed. Human life 'means' nothing. But that is not to say that it is not worth living. What does a Debussy *Arabesque* 'mean,' or a rainbow or a rose? A man delights in all of these, knowing himself to be no more—a wisp of music and a haze of dreams dissolving

against the sun. Man has only his own two feet to stand on, his own human trinity to see him through: Reason, Courage, and Grace. And the first plus the second equal the third." (pp. 166-67)

But a few days later Wanderhope's comfortable world begins to collapse. While he and Carol are on vacation in Bermuda, Carol's fever and back pains return. Wanderhope takes her home immediately, and Dr. Cameron gives her another blood test. This time it shows an elevated white count, and Dr. Cameron insists on a bone marrow test. The results aren't good: there is, as Dr. Cameron says, "a strong suggestion of leukemia." After delivering the painful prognosis, he moves briskly ahead:

"Now here's the thing. We have the world's leading authorities on its childhood forms right here in New York. You will take her in to Dr. Scoville tomorrow—"

"Can they do anything for it?"

"My dear boy, where have you been the last ten years? There are first of all the steroids—cortisone and ACTH— which give a quick remission. The minute she's pulled back to normal with those, Dr. Scoville will switch her to the first of the long-range drugs, some of which he's helped develop himself. If they should wear off, there's—but let's cross those bridges when we come to them. . . ."

"How long do these remissions last?"

The doctor described a circle so large the ice cubes rattled in his glass. "Years . . ."

"And by that time—"

"Of course! They're working on it day and night, and they're bound to get it soon." He jerked his head toward where he knew the telephone to be, and with an almost barroom-buddy solemnity said, "Chances are when I call Scoville to make an appointment for you he won't be home but at the laboratory with his rats. Oh, they'll get it! It's only a question of time, and that we've got on our side. As I say, ten years ago, nothing. Now a great deal. Look. Get this picture firmly fixed in your mind to the exclusion of everything else: *Carol going off to school again next September.* I promise it on my solemn oath." (pp. 169-70)

Scoville is indeed impressive, a man dedicated both to his patients and to attending research conferences on childhood leukemia. Like Dr. Cameron, he is brisk when he talks to Wanderhope, and he exhibits a similar enthusiasm for medical intervention and advances:

"The spleen is beginning to be felt, so the disease is coming along," he said, when we had both sat down. "Her hemoglobin is"—he consulted a paper a receptionist had put on his desk—"just a thousand. Down almost three hundred from the test Dr. Cameron ran Tuesday. So things are getting touch-and-go."

He laced his hands behind his head and blinked into the sunlight a moment.

"The two best drugs we have for acute leukemia are 6-mercaptopurine and Methotrexate. I'd like to start her on the 6-MP, but it needs a few weeks to take hold, and I don't know whether we have the time. She's pretty explosive. But let's try it. If things get tricky we'll just pop her into the hospital and dose her with cortisone. We like to keep the steroids for later, an ace in the hole, but if we need them now to pull her into shape for the 6-MP, we'll have to use them."

"What do you mean by things getting tricky?"

"Watch her for bleeding. What the disease does is destroy the platelets in the blood, which do our clotting for us. It's important she doesn't fall down or bump or cut herself in any way. No playgrounds or such till we get her into remission. If she goes to school, no gym, and tell the teacher to watch her."

"What shall I tell the teacher she has?"

"Say it's anemia. Tell Carol the same thing. That's part of it, after all. . . ."

"How long do the remissions last?"

"From the steroids, not long. From the other two drugs, anywhere from six months to a year or two. It's impossible to predict. About fifty per cent respond to the drugs."

"There are no cures?"

He smiled very tenderly across the desk. "That depends what you mean by a cure. I have a girl, now fifteen, who's been in the clear on 6-MP for over three years now. I'm sure in the end the cancer cells will develop a resistance to the drug."

"And then you'll switch to Methotrexate."

"And then we'll switch to Methotrexate."

"And by that time . . ."

"We hope so! Chemotherapy—drugs—is the scent we're on now, and it's only a few years ago we didn't have anything at all. It's quite a game of wits we're playing with this beast. The 6-MP, for example, breaks the cells up nutritionally by giving them counterfeit doses of the purine they like to gorge themselves on. I hope we'll have some other pranks to play on him soon, and if there are, you may be sure the clinic downstairs will be the first to try them out. There's nothing hot at the moment, but who knows? It's an exciting chase, though I can't expect you to look at it that way at the moment."

"Do you believe in God as well as play at him?"

"Between my work at the clinic and tearing around to every other hospital in the country, I sometimes go for weeks without seeing my own children. I have no time to think about such matters." (pp. 173-74)

Wanderhope now enters the world of illness: racing Carol back to the hospital so that she can be treated for a nosebleed; having her readmitted because the remission lasts only a short time; having her body ravaged by the tools necessary to "sustain" her. Horror becomes commonplace:

There was again the familiar scene: the mothers with their nearly dead, the false face of mercy, the Slaughter of the Innocents. A girl with one leg came unsteadily down the hall between crutches, skillfully encouraged by nurses. Through the pane in a closed door a boy could be seen sitting up in bed, bleeding from everything in his head; a priest lounged alertly against the wall, ready to move in closer. In the next room a boy of five was having Methotrexate pumped into his skull, or, more accurately, was watching a group of mechanics gathered solemnly around the stalled machine. . . .

Among the parents and children, flung together in a hell of prolonged farewell, wandered forever the ministering vampires from Laboratory, sucking samples from bones and veins to see how went with each the enemy that had marked them all. And the doctors in their butchers' coats, who severed the limbs and gouged the brains and knifed the vitals where the demon variously dwelt, what did they think of these best fruits of ten million hours of dedicated toil? They hounded the culprit from organ to organ and joint to joint till nothing remained over which to practice their art: the art of prolonging sickness. Yet medicine had its own old aphorism: "Life is a fatal disease." (pp. 205-6)

In order to sleep at night, Wanderhope masters "the art of remaining half drunk while having lost the joy of drink" (p. 176). Although he awakens "from nightmares to a nightmare" (p. 177), he does his best to enjoy every moment with Carol. It is a time of new intensity, a time of living each day to the hilt, and Wanderhope does his best to be the perfect father—to understand the complex rela-

tionship between Carol and Mrs. Brodhag, to support her
friendship with Omar Howard, the precocious neighbor boy.
Yet the intrusions of grim reality persist: Carol experiences
a succession of physical problems in response to and in spite
of the drugs she's dosed with—a huge appetite and weight
gain, the danger of high blood pressure, headaches, stinging
gums, eye trouble—the result of being kept on what Dr.
Scoville calls "the edge of toxicity" (p. 194) in the losing
battle to rout the leukemia. And when Carol is in the final
stages of the disease, one of the last drugs administered to
her in desperation causes her hair to fall out.

Sustaining Wanderhope are conversations with Stein,
another parent he meets at the hospital. Stein's daughter
Rachel is also dying of leukemia. Stein approaches her illness
with what Wanderhope describes as an attitude of "assertive
hopelessness"; he is unimpressed by all the research being
done to come up with the next miracle drug: " 'They'll never
get it, cancer. They'll never conquer it. Do you know what
it is, that sluggishly multiplying anarchy? A souvenir from
the primordial ooze. The original Chaos, without form and
void. In de beginning was de void, and de void was vit God.
Mustn't say de naughty void,' he finished in a sudden spasm
of burlesque that could only have revealed a man so full of
hate that he is prepared to turn it on himself" (p. 181). Yet
Stein is not without humanity; indeed, he is perhaps too
much imbued with it. This becomes clear one day when he
asks Wanderhope to join him for lunch. On the way they
pass the nearby church of St. Catherine of Siena, and they
begin talking about God and faith:

> "You don't believe in God," I said to Stein.
> "God is a word banging around in the human nervous
> system. He exists about as much as Santa Claus."

"Santa Claus has had a tremendous influence, exist or not."
"For children."
"Lots of saints have died for God with a courage that is hardly childish."
"That's part of the horror. It's all a fantasy. It's all for nothing. A martyr giving his life, a criminal taking one. It's all the same to the All."
"I can't believe that."
"Congratulations."
We fell into a gloomy but curiously companionable silence. I changed the subject by jerking my head once more toward the research building before we turned the corner out of its sight. "We've got that to be grateful for, maybe even pious about. Ten years ago our children wouldn't have stood a chance."
"So death by leukemia is now a local instead of an express. Same run, only a few more stops. But that's medicine, the art of prolonging disease."
"Jesus," I said, with a laugh. "Why would anybody want to prolong it?"
"In order to postpone grief." (pp. 182-83)

Wanderhope and Stein continue their argument through the multiple hospitalizations that Rachel and Carol, who become close friends, endure. One day the two men and Mrs. Stein come upon a touching sight: their daughters sitting side by side making paper flowers for "children less fortunate."

"Aren't they just too sweet together?" [Mrs. Stein] beamed in the doorway.
"Lifelong friends," said Stein, who gave, and asked, no quarter. (p. 214)

Wanderhope once observes to Stein that the debate they're having has been going on for centuries, and that "there's as much to be said for one side as for the other. Fifty-fifty." But Stein disagrees, noting that one point is decisive: "One charge can be brought against your point of view that can't against mine: wishful thinking. Believers believe what they want to believe. I would like to believe it, too, but deny that an honest man can. Unbelief is to that extent less suspect than faith" (p. 213). During this conversation they pass the church of St. Catherine, "from which a pair of people were contentedly emerging after their evening devotionals" (p. 213), and Stein reacts:

> Here a vibration of anger escaped Stein that was not put into words, but that I felt had given me a flash of illumination into his spirit—something that might even be held to confirm the theory of my friend to which I had been needled into giving audible expression. Stein resented the sedative power of religion, or rather the repose available to those blissfully ignorant that the medicament was a fictitious blank. In this exile from peace of mind to which his reason doomed him, he was like an insomniac driven to awaken sleepers from dreams illegitimately won by going around shouting, "Don't you realize it was a placebo!" Thus it seemed to me that what you were up against in Stein was not logic rampant, but frustrated faith. He could not forgive God for not existing. (pp. 213-14)

Looking back, Wanderhope muses, "My conversations with Stein are almost all I am recalling of my relations with other parents because they were vital to my concerns, not because they . . . were typical of human intercourse there. Far from it" (pp. 214-15). Most of the other parents passed the time with small talk, what we often take refuge in when we're terrified: "we chatter of this and that while our hearts

burn within us" (p. 215). There is a reason for this, Wanderhope says:

> We live this life by a kind of conspiracy of grace: the com-
> mon assumption, or pretense, that human existence is
> "good" or "matters" or has "meaning," a glaze of charm or
> humor by which we conceal from one another and perhaps
> even ourselves the suspicion that it does not, and our con-
> viction in times of trouble that it is overpriced—something
> to be endured rather than enjoyed. Nowhere does this func-
> tion more than in precisely such a slice of hell as a Children's
> Pavilion [a child-care unit in a hospital], where the basic
> truths would seem to mock any state of mind other than
> rage and despair. Rage and despair are indeed carried about
> in the heart, but privately, to be let out on special occasions,
> like savage dogs for exercise, occasions in solitude when God
> is cursed, birds stoned from the trees or the pillow ham-
> mered in darkness. In the ward lounge itself, a scene in
> which a changing collection of characters are waiting for a
> new medicine that might as well be called Godot, the con-
> versation is indistinguishable from that going on at the
> moment in the street, a coffee break at the office from which
> one is absent, or a dinner party to which one could not
> accept an invitation. Even the exchange of news about their
> children has often the quality of gossip. An earful of it would
> be incredible to an uninvolved spectator, not to its princi-
> pals. Quiet is requested for the benefit of the other parents.
> One holds his peace in obedience to a tacit law as binding
> as if it were framed on a corridor wall with a police officer
> on hand to see that it was enforced: "No fuss." This is all
> perhaps nothing more than the principle of sportsmanship
> at its highest, given in return for the next man's. Even Stein
> had it in no small degree, for all his seeming refusal to wish
> me good hunting in my spiritual quest. Perhaps he was
> trying to tell me in as nice a way as he could that there was

no game in those woods. His grim little jokes on the barricades were in their way part of this call to courage. (pp. 215-16)

For Wanderhope it finally ends more with a whimper than a bang. In desperation he has even gone and prayed at St. Catherine's, kneeling before the shrine to St. Jude, "Patron of Lost Causes and Hopeless Cases," and begging for a stay of execution: "Give us a year. We will spend it as we have the last, missing nothing" (p. 228). At first Wanderhope's prayer appears to be answered. When, as the more standard remedies begin to fail, Dr. Cameron tries an experimental drug on Carol, the results are good: Carol's bone marrow once again returns almost to normal, giving Wanderhope new hope. On the morning he's been told he can take Carol home again, Mrs. Brodhag bakes a cake for him to take to the hospital for Carol to enjoy at her birthday party before she returns home. On his way to the hospital, Wanderhope turns once again into St. Catherine's, boxed cake in hand, kneeling to pray. When he finishes, his hopes are suddenly dashed. The night nurse, Mrs. Morano, has come to say her morning prayers, and she tells him that Carol has developed an infection due to her depressed white count, which was brought on by the new drug. Wanderhope hurries to the hospital, where the news is grim:

One look at Carol and I knew it was time to say good-by. The invading germ, or germs, had not only ravaged her bloodstream by now, but had broken out on her body surface in septicemic discolorations. Her foul enemy had his will of her well at last. One of the blotches covered where they were trying to insert a catheter, and spread down along a thigh. By afternoon it had traveled to the knee, and by the next, gangrened. Dr. Scoville could not have been kinder.

"Someone has ordered another tank of oxygen," he told me that afternoon in the corridor, "but I think you'll agree it won't be necessary. . . . I've left orders for all the morphine she needs. She'll slip away quietly. She doesn't know us now. It's just as well, because there isn't much in the new drug, if it's any consolation. We have a co-operative study on it, and the remissions are few and brief, and suspect because of the incidence of Meticorten administered with it. We can never be sure it wasn't the Meticorten in this case. It would only have meant another short reprieve—no pardon." He sighed and went his busy way, to the ends of the earth. (pp. 232-33)

When the nurse leaves the room, Wanderhope whispers quickly to Carol, "The Lord bless thee, and keep thee: The Lord make his face shine upon thee, and be gracious unto thee: The Lord lift up his countenance upon thee, and give thee peace" (p. 234). Next he enacts a ritual of farewell:

Then I touched the stigmata one by one: the prints of the needles, the wound in the breast. . . . I caressed the perfectly shaped head. I bent to kiss the cheeks, the breasts that would now never be fulfilled. . . .

The lips curled in another smile. . . . It was the expression on her face when her homework was going well, the shine of pride at a column of figures mastered or a poem to spring successfully forged. (pp. 234-35)

A short while later, Carol dies, "borne from the dull watchers on a wave that broke and crashed beyond our sight" (p. 236). Stunned, Wanderhope retreats to the bar down the street and drinks until the bartender refuses to serve him any longer. When he leaves the bar he passes the church of St. Catherine, which reminds him that, in his haste to get to the hospital that morning, he had left Carol's cake there.

He goes inside and finds the cake in the pew where he had left it. Taking the cake outside, he turns to the crucified Christ hanging over the central doorway of the church and vents his pent-up rage and pain:

> Then my arm drew back and let fly with all the strength within me.
>
> It was miracle enough that the pastry should reach its target at all, at that height from the sidewalk. The more so that it should land squarely, just beneath the crown of thorns. Then through scalded eyes I seemed to see the hands free themselves of the nails and move slowly toward the soiled face. Very slowly, very deliberately, with infinite patience, the icing was wiped from the eyes and flung away. I could see it fall in clumps to the porch steps. Then the cheeks were wiped down with the same sense of grave and gentle ritual, with all the kind sobriety of one whose voice could be heard saying, "Suffer the little children to come unto me . . . for of such is the kingdom of heaven."
>
> Then the scene dissolved itself in a mist in which my legs could no longer support their weight, and I sank down to the steps. I sat on its worn stones, to rest a moment before going on. Thus Wanderhope was found at that place which for the diabolists of his literary youth, and for those with more modest spiritual histories too, was said to be the only alternative to the muzzle of a pistol: the foot of the Cross. (pp. 237-38)

Months later, after Wanderhope has put the house up for sale and is going through things in Carol's bedroom, he finds a tape Carol had made. It begins with some absurd dialogue between Wanderhope and Mrs. Brodhag, which Carol had mischievously recorded without the two of them knowing it. Next are some of Carol's favorite piano pieces, followed by a long silence. Just as Wanderhope reaches for the switch to turn the tape recorder off, he hears Carol's voice again. This time she has a message for him:

> I want you to know that everything is all right, Daddy. I mean you mustn't worry, really. You've helped me a lot— more than you can imagine. I was digging around in the cabinet part at the bottom of the bookshelves for something to read that you would like. I mean, not something from your favorite books of poetry and all, but something of your own. What did I come across but that issue of the magazine put out by your alma mater, with the piece in it about your philosophy of life. Do you remember it? I might as well say that I know what's going on. What you wrote gives me courage to face whatever there is that's coming, so what could be more appropriate than to read it for you now? . . . I don't understand it all, but I think I get the drift. (p. 241)

Carol then proceeds to read her father's critique of "those consolations called religious," in which he concludes, "Man has only his own two feet to stand on, his own human trinity to see him through" (p. 241).

Wanderhope is stunned to hear these words come back to him, at this time and in this way: "I reached the couch at last, on which I lay for some hours as though I had been clubbed, not quite to death. . . . Sometime [around morning] I went to my bedroom, where from a bureau drawer I drew a small cruciform trinket on a chain. I went outside, walking down the slope of back lawn to the privet hedge, over which I hurled it as far as I could into the trees beyond. They were the sacred wood where we had so often walked" (p. 242). His thoughts are bitter:

> How I hate this world. I would like to tear it apart with my own two hands if I could. I would like to dismantle the universe star by star, like a treeful of rotten fruit. Nor do I

believe in progress. . . . Progress doubles our tenure in a vale of tears. . . . Man is inconsolable, thanks to that eternal "Why?" when there is no Why, that question mark twisted like a fishhook in the human heart. "Let there be light," we cry, and only the dawn breaks.

What are these thoughts? They are the shadow, no doubt, reaching out to declare me my father's son. But before that I shall be my daughter's father. Not to say my brother's brother. Now through the meadows of my mind wander hand in hand Louie and Carol and at last little Rachel, saying, "My grace is sufficient for thee." For we are indeed saved by grace in the end—but to give, not take. This, it seems then, is my Book of the Dead. All I know I have learned from them—my long-suffering mother and my crazy father, too, and from Greta, gone frowning somewhere, her secret still upon her brow. All I am worth I got from them. And Rena too, and Dr. Simpson's little boy. . . .

I could not decline the burden of resumption. The Western Gate is closed. That exit is barred. One angel guards it, whose sword is a gold head smiling into the sun in a hundred snapshots. The child on the brink of whose grave I tried to recover the faith lost on the edge of my brother's is the goalkeeper past whom I can now never get. In the smile are sealed my orders for the day. One has heard of people being punished for their sins, hardly for their piety. But so it is. As to that other One, whose voice I thought I heard, I seem to be barred from everything it speaks in comfort, only the remonstrance remaining: "Verily I say unto thee, Thou shalt by no means come out thence, till thou has paid the uttermost farthing." (pp. 243-44)

Wanderhope ends his tale with some exquisitely painful observations:

Time heals nothing—which should make us the better able to minister. There may be griefs beyond the reach of solace, but none worthy of the name that does not set free the springs of sympathy. Blessed are they that comfort, for they too have mourned, may be more likely the human truth. "You had a dozen years of perfection. That's a dozen more than most people get," a man had rather sharply told me one morning on the train. He was the father of one of Carol's classmates, a lumpish girl of no wiles and no ways, whose Boston mother had long since begun to embalm her dreams in alcohol. . . . Once I ran into Carol's teacher, Miss Halsey. "Some poems are long, some are short. She was a short one," Miss Halsey had summed up, smiling, with the late-Gothic horse face which guarantees that she will never read any poems, long or short, to any children of her own. Again the throb of compassion rather than the breath of consolation: the recognition of how long, how long is the mourners' bench upon which we sit, arms linked in un-deluded friendship, all of us, brief links, ourselves, in the eternal pity. (p. 246)

On Getting the Issues Right: A Commentary

I have tried to tell the story that DeVries tells in his novel with as little commentary as possible. Of course, you can-not tell the story of the novel without commentary, particu-larly if you have chosen, as I have, to summarize the story, thus fundamentally distorting DeVries's telling of Don Wanderhope's telling of the story. Just as the novel itself is a distortion of the experience, so I have distorted the distor-tion. But perhaps the whole language of distortion is a mis-take. For there is no experience without mediation by a story. There is no primal experience of God, of suffering, or even of the death of a child. So I hope my distortion, if it be that, helps us get at what bothers us so deeply about the suffering and death of a child and why we think that has implications for our belief in God; or, better put, perhaps through the retelling of this story we will better understand how our belief in God entails that we suffer with a suffering child.

Of course, one of the reasons I chose to use DeVries's story is that in it he uses the prismatic power of the novel to place one man's struggle with belief and unbelief in close proximity with the suffering and death of a child. Equally important is our being able to see the struggle to cure Carol through the agency of medicine. Because we identify with Wanderhope, DeVries can lead us along the path that Wanderhope walks, the path that strips us of easy answers and false comforts. In short, we are put in a position to begin, rightly, to raise questions about the suffering of children like Carol.

The power of *The Blood of the Lamb* derives from De-Vries's refusal to clarify the ambiguities of Wanderhope's character and/or to resolve the major dilemma of the action. We are never sure if Wanderhope believes or does not believe. Like most of us, whether we be convinced believers or unbelievers, Wanderhope wanders between unbelief and belief, unsure what difference either makes. We are not sure, as Wanderhope himself is not sure, how to understand a person who can write "Human life 'means' nothing," and yet cannot stay out of St. Catherine's. What is interesting about Wanderhope is not whether he explicitly believes or not, but what he does. Like his father, Wanderhope swims in the sea of faith—that is, he is surrounded by the storied habits of a people whose way of life is so God-determined that even their unbelief is a form of faithfulness.

Wanderhope gives some indication that he understands

this when, early in the novel, he reports a comic scene between Ben, his father; Louie, his brother; and his Uncle Hans. Ben and Hans are having their usual debate about the Bible when Louie observes that "the virgin birth business was slipped in by a later writer, prolly" (p. 6). Louie then goes on to instruct his stunned "congregation," which includes his mother and grandmother, that once you no longer believe the Bible is infallible, "you can begin to appreciate it as great literature" (p. 7). "The Book of Job," he says, "is the greatest drama ever struck off by the hand of man. Just terrific theater. Greater than Aeschylus, prolly" (pp. 7-8). This observation draws dramatic responses from Louie's audience: "Our mother was wiping the table with one hand and her eyes with the other. Our father . . . seemed to be trying to extricate his head from his hands as from a porthole, or vise, into which it had been inadvertently thrust. My uncle put his face up close to Louie's and said, 'You're talking to a servant of God!'" (p. 8).

Wanderhope offers this gloss on the scene:

Such a scene may seem, to households devoid of polemic excitement, to lie outside credulity, but it was a common one in ours. Now when I am myself no longer assailed by doubts, being rather lashed by certainties, I can look back on it with a perspective quite lacking in my view of it then, for my teeth were chattering. We were a chosen people, more so than the Jews, who had "rejected the cornerstone," our concept of Calvinist election reinforced by that of Dutch supremacy. My mother even then sometimes gave the impression that she thought Jesus was a Hollander. Not that our heroes did not include men of other extractions and other faiths. Several years after the Scopes trial, we were still aggressively mourning the defeat of William Jennings Bryan. (pp. 8-9)

When you have a mother who thinks that Jesus may have been a Hollander, atheism is not really a possibility. You may be angry at God, but to approach life without a sense of destiny, without a sense that there is more to this life than to eat, get laid, and die, is impossible for a Wanderhope. That is why Wanderhope cannot stay away from St. Catherine's or from confronting God before the altar of St. Jude. Soon after Carol has been diagnosed with leukemia, Wanderhope and Mrs. Brodhag rush her to the hospital when she develops a nosebleed. Once Carol is being attended to, Wanderhope follows Mrs. Brodhag into St. Catherine's, where, despite the fact that she is "a Congregationalist habituated to plain interiors," she kneels to pray. Wandering through the church, Wanderhope finds himself before the shrine to St. Jude; there he "sank to the floor and, squeezing wet eyes to hands clenched into one fist, uttered the single cry, 'No!'" (p. 176).

After Carol has been hospitalized innumerable times, Wanderhope finds himself back in St. Catherine's, "deaddrunk and stone-sober and bone-tired." Once again dying to learn but dreading to hear whether this or that drug will produce the slim thread of hope called remission, he again prays before St. Jude, "Patron of Lost Causes and Hopeless Cases." It is a prayer I cited part of earlier, but one that warrants quoting in its entirety:

> I do not ask that she be spared to me, but that her life be spared to her. Or give us a year. We will spend it as we have the last, missing nothing. We will mark the dance of every hour between the snowdrop and the snow: crocus to tulip to violet to iris to rose. We will note not only the azalea's crimson flowers but the red halo that encircles a while the azalea's root when her petals are shed, also the

white halo that rings for a week the foot of the old catalpa tree. Later we will prize the chrysanthemums which last so long, almost as long as paper flowers, perhaps because they know in blooming not to bloom. We will seek out the leaves turning in the little-praised bushes and the unadvertised trees. Everyone loves the sweet, neat blossom of the hawthorn in spring, but who lingers over the olive drab of her leaf in autumn? We will. We will note the lost yellows in the tangles of that bush that spills over the Howards' stone wall, the meek hues among which it seems to hesitate before committing itself to red, and next year learn its name. We will seek out these modest subtleties so lost in the blare of oaks and maples, like flutes and woodwinds drowned in brasses and drums. When winter comes, we will let no snow fall ignored. We will again watch the first blizzard from her window like figures locked snug in a glass paperweight. "Pick one out and follow it to the ground!" she will say again. We will feed the plain birds that stay to cheer us through the winter, and when spring returns we shall be the first out, to catch the snowdrop's first white whisper in the wood. All this we ask, with the remission of our sins, in Christ's name. Amen. (pp. 228-29)

A few days after Wanderhope offers this prayer, Carol is dead.

DeVries does not resolve Wanderhope's pain before God. He does not say—and I think he is right in so refraining—that Wanderhope through Carol's suffering has learned to see the beauty in the olive drab of the hawthorn in autumn. DeVries is too wise for that, sensing as he does the dishonesty in those who would have a child like Carol suffer and die from leukemia so that a father like Wanderhope could learn to see the particular beauty of the everyday. Even more cruel would be one who believes that a God worthy of worship would use the suffering of a child like Carol to make a Wanderhope "more religious."

Of course, we see that Wanderhope ends up at the foot of the cross under a Jesus crying tears of cake frosting. The suggestion is that Wanderhope is comforted by a God who suffers with us, who can share our agonies—who has, in short, become like us. There is no hope for us if our only hope in the face of suffering is that "we can learn from it," or that we can use what we learn from the treatment of that suffering to overcome eventually what has caused it (e.g., many children in the future will be helped by what we have learned by using experimental drugs on children like Carol), or that we can use suffering to organize our energies to mount effective protests against oppression. Rather, our only hope lies in whether we can place alongside the story of the pointless suffering of a child like Carol a story of suffering that helps us know we are not thereby abandoned. This, I think, is to get the question of "theodicy" right, a point that I will develop further in the next chapter.

By suggesting that Wanderhope is "comforted" by finding himself at the foot of a cake-drenched Jesus, I do not mean that he is or should be any less angry about Carol's death. Moreover, the novel ends with Wanderhope's comment that all we can gain from our suffering is a sense of compassion for one another's hurt—that we are all sitting on a mourners' bench that is longer than we had imagined. Such a response to the suffering of a child like Carol can be but an extremely attractive and humane form of unbelief. According to this response—and it is not a response that can be easily dismissed—in the absence of God the best we can do is comfort one another in the loneliness and the silences created by our suffering.

There are no quick or easy responses which can show

that such compassion is unintelligible in a world devoid of God. As I shall try to show, it is not a question of whether the world or our compassion makes sense without God, but rather what kind of God it is Christians worship that makes intelligible our cry of rage against the suffering and death of our children. Put in terms of *The Blood of the Lamb,* the question is this: Why is it that Wanderhope, in spite of a life that is filled with disaster, never ceases to hope? Why, in short, does he have hope sufficient to have a child in a world where at best he is only a wanderer—a Dutchman without a home, never to be accepted, forever a garbageman with a crazy father and a self-destructive wife? Is the inherent "meaning" of "a Debussy *Arabesque* . . . or a rainbow or a rose" (p. 167) sufficient to sustain that hope? If belief in God has nothing to do with such questions, then surely it makes little difference whether anyone believes or not—or worse, any belief we have cannot help but be an illusion that provides comfort that can only be false, self-deceptive, and serve oppressive powers.

To ask the question in this way, moreover, forces us to confront a more complex set of issues than "theodicies" normally entail. As I noted earlier, questions of "suffering" are not "eternal" but rather are always historically situated. *The Blood of the Lamb* makes clear that our questions about suffering are asked from a world determined by a hope schooled by medicine—a world that promises to "solve" suffering by eliminating its causes. Wanderhope's whole existence is determined by people associated with medicine and institutions that medicine has created: Louie, the brother he admired, who was going to be a doctor; ineffectual Doc Berkenbosch, who turned no one away, not even those who couldn't pay; Dr. Simpson, who hovered over those dying of tuberculosis; Dr. Cameron, who could refer one to the best specialists available; and finally Dr. Scoville, who had no time for questions about God. Obviously medicine becomes more pervasive in Wanderhope's life than Calvinism once was to Hollanders.

Why and how did this happen? Why did Wanderhope—who trusted few people and no church—trust the power of medicine, and how do we trust this new power to which we unquestioningly entrust our children in the hope that they will be made better? It may be true that we no longer trust in God to heal our children, but the interesting question is why we put so much trust in medicine. This seems particularly puzzling when we realize that most of us know even less about medicine than we once did about God.

It has long been pointed out by sociologists of religion that the function of theodicies, and indeed of religion itself, is to explain human suffering by reference to a sacred order that legitimates our institutions. In that respect the sacred order we see called into question in a novel like *The Blood of the Lamb* is not that of Dutch Calvinism but that of science and medicine. It is the world of science that teaches us to explain illness and suffering as the result of physical processes that have gone wrong. All that is required to make our world right is the increasing development of our intelligence and knowledge. In the name of that development we are now ready to offer up our children to the priests of this new hope, believing as we do that finally a "cure" will be found.

So the issue for our time cannot simply be the relation between our belief in God and the suffering of a child like Carol, but how the God in which we ought to believe should make a difference for the way in which we understand the nature and function of medicine. What we may well have is the conflict between two contending "theodicies," both with their own patterns of legitimation that may be equally perverse. Why, for example, is Wanderhope so willing to continue to give Carol up to the suffering prolonged by medicine when he would have been resistant to any notion that Carol might have to suffer and even die for the God found at St. Catherine's?

It is important that we not think this is a matter of pitting science against religion because the issues are far too serious for such games. It is not a question of winners and losers but rather a question of why we place such desperate faith in medicine. Behind this question, of course, lies the even more challenging question of why we are so disturbed by the death of our children and would willingly subject them to prolonged agony rather than face their deaths.

Wanderhope faced much in his life—the death of his brother; the insanity and death of his father; the death of his girlfriend, Rena; the suicide of his wife, Greta. Yet none of these bothered him like Carol's death. What is it about the suffering and death of a child that seems to challenge not only our belief in God but also our very hold on existence? The suffering and death of Wanderhope's father was no less real. Does the mere fact that adults have had a shot at life make that much difference in our attitude about the pointless suffering and untimely deaths of those who are no longer children?

In order to try to get a handle on this question, we will need to explore whether there are different kinds of suffering and on what basis such discriminations are made. Just as our belief in God is historically situated, so is our account of suffering. Don Wanderhope not only swam in the sea of Dutch Calvinism; he also assumed that the suffering of children was of a different order than that of adults like Rena and Greta. If we are to understand the challenge of suffering, we will need to try to understand why we share that assumption with him.

Finally, we need to reflect on the fact that the story of Don Wanderhope is just that—a story. We have already noted that the novel seems to end inconclusively. However, does the very fact that the story was told, that Don and Carol's suffering was narrated, affect our capacity to absorb the pain of Carol's death? Can the story be told without the telling of it domesticating the rage we should feel at her death? To answer such questions, we must consider our understanding of God and our understanding of suffering and the possible relation between these two things.

CHAPTER II

Theology, Theodicy, and Medicine

Why Theodicy Is Not a Problem

The problem with atheism is that it is not a problem."[1] A strange claim, to be sure, but one I think true. The same is true of the problem of evil—it simply is not always and everywhere "a" problem that makes sense from "anyone's" point of view. The problem, of course, is in the articles "a" and "the." Obviously the illnesses and deaths of Carol Wanderhopes are a challenge to all that we hold dear, including our relation to God. By denying that there is a problem of evil I am not trying to defeat the cry of pain we should feel at the death of a child. Rather, I am trying to remind us that theodicy is basically a parasitic endeavor that draws its life from more positive modes of life.

Michael Buckley makes this point well in his magisterial book entitled *At the Origins of Modern Atheism,* when

---

1. Michael J. Buckley, S.J., *At the Origins of Modern Atheism* (New Haven: Yale University Press, 1987), p. 13.

he observes that "the central meaning of atheism is not to be sought immediately in atheism; it is to be sought in those gods or that god affirmed, which atheism has either engaged or chosen to ignore as beneath serious challenge. The history of the term indicates this constant, and the analysis of its meaning suggests that it is inescapable: atheism is essentially parasitic."[2] Without the theist, atheism is irrelevant.

Accordingly, Buckley argues that modern atheism is a genuinely new phenomenon: the god which the modern atheist denied—that is, the god of Descartes and Newton that d'Holbach and Diderot denied—was a strange god created by attempts to show that god could be proven or known on philosophical grounds alone. Buckley comments,

> The extraordinary note about this emergence of the denial of the Christian god which Nietzsche celebrated is that Christianity as such, more specifically the person and teaching of Jesus or the experience and history of the Christian Church, did not enter the discussion. The absence of any consideration of Christology is so persvasive throughout serious discussion that it becomes taken for granted, yet it is so stunningly curious that it raises a fundamental issue of the modes of thought: How did the issue of Christianity vs. atheism become purely philosophical? To paraphrase Tertullian: How was it that the only arms to defend the temple were to be found in the Stoa?[3]

For our purposes it is not necessary to follow Buckley's extraordinary history of how it happened that Christian theologians, when confronted by modern atheism, had at their disposal only a god which lacked any characteristics of a Trini-

---

2. Buckley, *At the Origins of Modern Atheism*, p. 15.
3. Buckley, *At the Origins of Modern Atheism*, p. 33.

tarian God that can save. What is important for our purposes
is to note that the assumption that there is something called
the problem of evil which creates a discourse called "theodicy"
occurred at the same time that modern atheism came into
being. The creation of "the" problem of evil is a correlative
of the creation of a god that, it was presumed, could be known
separate from a community of people at worship.[4]

It no doubt seems strange and overintellectualistic,
especially after we have just finished examining a story like
The Blood of the Lamb, to be told that the problem with the

---

4. In *Theology and the Problem of Evil* (Oxford: Basil Blackwell,
1986), Kenneth Surin quotes Walter Kasper to characterize philosophical
theism as "the abstract theism of a unipersonal God who stands over
against man as the perfect Thou or over man as imperial ruler and judge."
According to Surin, "Kasper finds this modern philosophical theism to
be ultimately untenable for a number of reasons":

> For one thing, if we imagine God as the other-worldly counterpart
> of man, then despite all the personal categories we use we will
> ultimately think of him in objectivist terms as a being who is
> superior to other beings. When this happens, God is being con-
> ceived as a finite entity who comes in conflict with finite reality
> and the modern understanding of it. Then we must either conceive
> God at the expense of man and the world, or conceive the world
> at the expense of God, thus limiting God in deistic fashion and
> finally eliminating him entirely with the atheists. This conversion
> of theism into a-theism also takes place for another reason: theism
> almost necessarily falls under the suspicion voiced by the critics
> of religion, that the theistic God is a projection of the human ego
> and a hypostatized idol, or that theism is ultimately a form of
> idolatry.

Surin notes that "it is certainly no exaggeration to say that vir-
tually every contemporary discussion of the theodicy-question is prem-
ised, implicitly or explicitly, on an understanding of 'God' overwhelm-
ingly constrained by the principles of *seventeenth and eighteenth century*
philosophical theism" (p. 4).

problem of evil is that the issue presupposes that the question of God's existence can be separated from God's character, but I hope to show that this is the heart of the matter. This is not Don Wanderhope's problem, because he had the advantage of not having received the miseducation in modern theology and philosophy that might have created for him the problem of evil. Yet these issues are not irrelevant to his story, because the same conditions that create modern atheism and theodical speculation also have Don Wanderhope—and us—in their grip.

Why this is so can be illumined by attending to Walter Brueggemann's understanding of theodicy and the Psalms. In *The Message of the Psalms* Brueggemann observes,

> The conventional idea of theodicy concerns God in relation to evil. If God is *powerful* and *good,* how can there be evil in the world? If the question is posed in this way, religion can offer no adequate logical response. Logically one must compromise either God's power or God's love, either saying that evil exists because God is not powerful enough to overrule it, or because God is not loving enough to use God's power in this way. To compromise in either direction is religiously inadequate and offers no satisfying response. Today the theological discussion seems to insist on holding on to God's love even at the risk of God's sovereign power. What faith offers is a sense of trust that is prepared to submit. That deep trust summons us to hard rethinking about the categories in which we do our reflection.[5]

According to Brueggemann, "The characteristic way of handling theodicy in Old Testament scholarship, and in the

---

5. Brueggemann, *The Message of the Psalms: A Theological Commentary* (Minneapolis: Augsburg Publishing House, 1984), p. 169.

theological enterprise more generally, is to see that the question becomes acute in Israel in the 7th-6th centuries B.C.E., around the collapse of Jerusalem, temple, and dynasty."[6] In short, the question arises not out of an experience of suffering in general, but against the background of Israel's faith in a God who had covenanted with her, giving her a destiny that seemed to promise glory. The loss of Israel's control over her political destiny, therefore, called into question "the old theories (Deuteronomic and sapiential) that good people prosper and evil people suffer."[7] A whole literature developed, of which the book of Job is best known, probing the question of God's justice.

This approach has the virtue of seeing that the question of God's justice can be posed only against the background of a community's tradition. For example, we would not even know what it means for God to be just if Israel had not been rescued from Egypt. Yet Brueggemann notes that such an approach is still too narrow because it continues to presuppose the legitimacy of the "conventional idea of theodicy" as the question of God's relation to evil.

> Though the question [of God's justice] grows out of historical experience and finds literary expression, it is treated as a theological question without any serious attention to other payoff systems of reward and punishment that are practiced in political and economic ways. But serious theodicy is always linked to social arrangements of access and benefit. . . . The question of theodicy is never a narrow religious question. It must be understood sociologically as a question about law, about the rule of law, about the reliability of the system of rewards and punishments. Theodicy then concerns

---

6. Brueggemann, *The Message of the Psalms,* p. 169.
7. Brueggemann, *The Message of the Psalms,* p. 169.

the character of God as practiced in the system of values in a social matrix.[8]

While I am in essential agreement with Brueggemann's point, I find it interesting that he describes concern for God's relation to evil as "conventional theodicy." In an odd way that is to accept recent developments—that is, developments in the seventeenth and eighteenth centuries—as normative for defining the issue. To do so, moreover, is to accept the assumption that theodical questions are timeless and thus unchanging. But it is this assumption that must be challenged if we are to appreciate the significance of Brueggemann's point that questions of evil cannot be divorced from the power structures of the social situation they reflect. The crucial question for us is what system of power is operative in our assumption that suffering makes God's existence qua existence doubtful, and how does that system shake the world of Don and Carol Wanderhope?

In *God and Human Suffering,* Douglas John Hall rightly argues that the "conventional" manner of putting the question creates problems:

> Such a formulation of the question . . . obscures its most existential dimension, which is the identity and condition of the one who asks it. The poem of Job is a paradigmatic and unforgettable grappling with the problem of God and human suffering because it is *not* theoretical, but a drama in which the identity of all those who put the question, especially Job himself, is revealed in detail. It is because Job is who he is that the question is put in the way that it is put, and that "the answer" must be given in the form in which it is given.

---

8. Brueggemann, *The Message of the Psalms,* p. 170.

No human question is ever asked (and no answer given!) in a historical vacuum; it is asked in a specific time and place by specific persons. With certain kinds of questions this contextual dimension may not be so significant; but with our present question it is of primary importance. The aspects of the problem of suffering which we shall hold up, as well as the responses that we shall give to them, will be determined in great measure by the particular circumstances, openly acknowledged or silently assumed, in which we find ourselves.[9]

Of course, if Hall is right about this, and I think he is, it may well mean that it is a mistake to characterize the book of Job as "grappling with the problem of God and human suffering." To make the book of Job, and especially God's answer to Job out of the whirlwind, an answer to the problem of evil is to try to make the book answer a question it was not asking.[10] Hall, I think, well understands this, since he

---

9. Hall, *God and Human Suffering: An Exercise in the Theology of the Cross* (Minneapolis: Augsburg Publishing House, 1986), p. 24.

10. For an extraordinary account of Job that takes seriously the ironic form of the book as intrinsic to its theology, see *Job* by J. Gerald Janzen (Atlanta: John Knox Press, 1985). In "God and the Silencing of Job" (*Modern Theology* 5 [Apr. 1989]), Terry Tilley argues,

Serious readers of Job have a choice. They can either read Job as silencing the voice of the suffering or allow Job to silence claims about how God and suffering are related. The book of Job displays the cost of providing the "systematic totalization" a theodicy requires: silencing the voice of the sufferer, even if she/he curses the day she/he was born and accuses God of causing human suffering, Job shows the theodicists' place is in the company of comforters, "delivering" their answers to those who are plagued with questions. . . . The comforters are "academics" in the worst sense of that term, ineffective observers of the terrors of human suffering, or tormenters who intensify that suffering by the ways they re-

notes that it makes not some difference but all the difference
who asks the question and why. For example, it makes all
the difference in the world whether the question of suffering
is asked by those who are actually suffering—those who are
dying from hunger, those who have to watch their children
die from diseases easily cured in developed countries. It is
one thing for theologians in the Third World to insist that
"while suffering is certainly real it is not ultimate"; it is quite
another thing for those of us in America to do so—and then
to assume that Job is asking the same question we are.[11] The
significance of this point has to be appreciated if we are to
rightly understand why the "conventional idea of theodicy"
is so distorting for Christian theological discourse and life.
As Brueggemann argues (drawing on the sociological insights
of Max Weber and Peter Berger), theodicy, despite its seemingly theoretical character, is a legitimation for the way in
which society is organized:

---

spond to suffering. Job reveals the worth of such academic responses to real evil. Perhaps the better alternative is for the reader
to remain silent. Readers may fear Job for good reason. The book
of Job makes no coherent claims. It provides no warrant for speaking of God or the meaning of human suffering. As a text for
scholarly inquiry, its scramblings, ambiguities and uncertainties
suggest that closure of the meaning of texts or canonization of a
"final" text may not be possible. As part of the Jewish and Christian religious canons, it reveals that no way of speaking of God
and suffering will do. As part of the cultural canon of the West,
it shows the hypocrisy of neglecting suffering when standing
outside the realm of suffering and telling the victims how they
could solve their problems. The comfortable alternative to listening to Job is usually preferred by literary-critical theological and
liturgical comforters: to play God and silence the voices of Job.
(pp. 267-68)

11. Hall, *God and Human Suffering*, pp. 24-25.

The practical effect is that theodicy is a theory of power about who makes decisions and who obeys them, who administers and controls good, who has access to them and on what terms. Or said another way, theodicy is an agreement about world-definition, about who gets to have a say, about who the authoritative interpreters are, and whose definitions and interpretations are "true" in this community. Theodicy is about the legitimacy of one's view of the world. . . . It is correct that there is no *crisis* in theodicy, but that is a *consensus* about theodicy all the same. Theodicy operates in times of equilibrium, as well as in times of crisis, but it is often hidden. We are agreed, and so we instruct our children, that this is the order to be honored and obeyed. We objectify and reify that order in a positivistic way, so that there is no room outside the consensus from which to mount a criticism. Obviously such an accepted theodicy is a form of social control and conformity. There is no crisis, but there is a theodicy, conventionally legitimated by the rule of God.[12]

Hall examines the "conventional idea of theodicy" in *God and Human Suffering* from another angle:

Formulating the problem of suffering in its conventional statement revolves around the seeming contradiction between the divine power and the divine love. If God is *loving* and at the same time *all-powerful,* then why is there so much suffering in the world? The assumption is that the deity *could,* if the deity *would,* simply eliminate suffering.

When the question is put in this way there is, I think, no satisfactory way of addressing it. The chance of there being a convincing response to such a formulation of the problem is at least severely limited; and the limiting factor is just this power assumption. When infinite power is

---

12. Brueggemann, *The Message of the Psalms,* pp. 170-71.

posited as the primary and characteristic attribute of deity, then no one can be satisfied with an answer that is less than the abolition of suffering as such![13]

That is not to say that the god of infinite power does not serve theodical purposes in Brueggemann's sense of theodicy. Ironically, this god of infinite power, the god that Kenneth Surin describes as the God of "philosophical theism,"[14] becomes the god that legitimates the Enlightenment project of extending human power over all contingency. Although this seems contradictory, in fact the view of an all-powerful but basically deistic god fits nicely with the understanding of the necessity of humankind's taking control of its destiny. If god cannot eliminate suffering, even though god may have the power to do so, then we will have to do god's task to insure that god can remain god.

This understanding of our existence and god often is presupposed by those of us who explicitly worship the God who suffered on the cross. For example, Alasdair MacIntyre has pointed out "the fact that the contradictions of a benevolent divine omnipotence and the existence of evil were not seen by the Christian thinkers of the Middle Ages as an obstacle to belief." Only after the seventeenth century did the problem of evil become the central challenge to "the coherence and intelligibility of Christian belief per se."[15] Accordingly, MacIntyre raises this question: "Why do the same intellectual difficulties at one time appear as difficulties but no more, an incentive to enquiry but not a ground for disbelief, while at another time they appear as a final and

---

13. Hall, *God and Human Suffering*, p. 97.

14. Surin, *Theology and the Problem of Evil*, pp. 3-7.

15. MacIntyre, quoted by Surin in *Theology and the Problem of Evil*, p. 9.

sufficient ground for scepticism and for the abandonment of Christianity?" Answering his own question, he suggests, "The apparent incoherence of Christian concepts was taken to be tolerable (and treated as apparent and not real) because the concepts were part of a set of concepts which were indispensable to the forms of description used in social and intellectual life."[16] That Christians now think the problem of suffering renders their faith in God unintelligible indicates that they now are determined by ways of life that are at odds with their fundamental convictions.

For the early Christians, suffering and evil, which for present purposes I do not need to distinguish, did not have to be "explained." Rather, what was required was the means to go on even if the evil could not be "explained." Indeed, it was crucial that such suffering or evil not be "explained" — that is, it was important not to provide a theoretical account of why such evil needed to be in order that certain good results occur, since such an explanation would undercut the necessity of the community capable of absorbing the suffering. "In an identifiably Christian context," says Kenneth Surin, "the 'problem of evil' arises (at least in part) when *particular* narratives of events of pain, dereliction, anguish, oppression, torture, humiliation, degradation, injustice, hunger, godforsakenness, and so on, come into collision with the Christian community's narratives, which are inextricably bound up with the redeeming reality of the triune God."[17]

In an attempt to help us understand the contrast between how the issue of evil works within the framework of Christian presuppositions and how it works within the

---

16. MacIntyre, quoted by Surin in *Theology and the Problem of Evil,* p. 9.

17. Surin, *Theology and the Problem of Evil,* p. 27.

framework of Enlightenment presuppositions, Surin calls attention to Augustine's understanding of evil. For Augustine, the problem of evil must be seen against the background of the goal of every Christian, which is "the attainment of blessedness," the way God has made possible through Jesus Christ. Ironically, the problem of evil can be located rightly when we understand that we are beings who were created to enjoy our status as creatures but who refuse to accept the gifts necessary for such joy. Therefore, the only hope for a resolution to our evil lies in the free gift of a gracious God. "So it is conversion—which comes about when the human will cooperates with divine grace—that solves the 'problem of evil,'" says Surin. "The unconverted person's endeavors to resolve the 'problem of evil,' no matter how sincere and intellectually gifted this person might be, are doomed ultimately to be self-defeating. Only faith in Christ makes possible the cleansing of our vision, a cleansing regarded by Augustine as the necessary preliminary to the vision of God." Without such conversion, "the very *process* of seeking to answer the question 'whence is evil?' will be undermined by the distorted thinking of a crippled intellect."[18]

According to Surin, Augustine's account of evil and the process of conversion must be supplemented by taking account of Augustine's historical context. Augustine, after all, was writing soon after Constantine legalized the Christian religion, a time when Christians were no longer being martyred but were enjoying positions of privilege. Accordingly, enemies of Christianity would no longer be "without"; they would be "within." Moreover, the "problem of evil" so conceived must be seen against Augustine's theology of history,

---

18. Surin, *Theology and the Problem of Evil*, p. 11.

which attempts to see the whole of history as the outworking of God's providence.[19]

Whatever flaws Augustine's account of evil has, and I think it has many, Augustine nonetheless sees the problem of evil as a practical problem. In this respect he continues to think of suffering from a Pauline perspective—as an opportunity for living in a way more faithful to the new age. Paul articulates this perspective in Romans 5: "Therefore, since we are justifed by faith, we have peace with God through our Lord Jesus Christ. Through him we have obtained access to this grace in which we stand, and we rejoice in our hope of sharing the glory of God. More than that, we rejoice in our sufferings, knowing that suffering produces endurance, and endurance produces character, and character produces hope, and hope does not disappoint us, because God's love has been poured into our hearts through the Holy Spirit which has been given to us" (vv. 1-5). Apparently it never occurred to the early Christians to question their belief in God or even God's goodness because they were unjustly suffering for their beliefs. Rather, their faith gave them direction in the face of persecution and general misfortune. Suffering was not a metaphysical problem needing a solution but a practical challenge requiring a response.

Therefore, the so-called problem of evil is not and cannot be a single problem, for it makes all the difference which god one worships as well as how one thinks that god is known. In contrast to Augustine's understanding of the problem of evil, the modern understanding of it is that it entails a theoretical enterprise which entertains the possibility of the existence of an omnipotent God. As Surin suggests, the subject who now asks the question about evil

---

19. Surin, *Theology and the Problem of Evil*, p. 12.

e putatively rational and autonomous individual who
co... *nes* herself [or himself] to the entirely *worldly* discipline
of 'evidencing' and 'justifying' cognitive formations, formations which, moreover, are restrictively derived from reason
and sense-experience. This worldly discipline, which finds
its authoritative manifestation in common-sense rationalism
and empiricism, would cease to be what it essentially is if
it were required to posit a subject whose self-definition
required her [or him] to *live* and *think* as a 'servant of
God.'"[20]

Theodicy done in this theoretical mode abstracts the
so-called problem of evil from any theological account of
history. Instead, Surin points out, theodicy is seen "as an
ahistorical and individualistic quest for logically stable notions, exact axioms, and rigorous chains of deductive infer-
ence. Unlike Augustine, the post-Leibnizian theodicist does
not feel constrained to understand history as *anything* possessing an intrinsic *thematic* importance, let alone as a
history which is the work of the very God who reveals
himself in Jesus Christ, and which is a determining ele-
ment in the subject's self-definition."[21] The "philosophical
theism" which generates the assumption that there is a
thing called the "problem of evil" has little in common
with the perspective of pre-Enlightenment theologians,
who saw the problem of suffering as a practical challenge
for the Christian community.

For Christians, suffering—even the suffering of a
child—cannot be separated from their calling to be a new
people made holy by conversion. "In a properly Christian
context," says Surin, "conversion is inseparable from fellow-

---

20. Surin, *Theology and the Problem of Evil*, p. 13.
21. Surin, *Theology and the Problem of Evil*, p. 13.

ship, a fellowship which is at root fellowship with . . . the Trinity itself. This fellowship is inseparable from commitment to a community, a commitment expressed in sharing its way of life, its customs and practices."[22] So, historically speaking, Christians have not had a "solution" to the problem of evil. Rather, they have had a community of care that has made it possible for them to absorb the destructive terror of evil that constantly threatens to destroy all human relations.

It is clear that something has gone decisively wrong for Christians when we underwrite the widespread assumption that there is a so-called problem of evil which is intelligible from anyone's perspective—that is, when we turn the Christian faith into a system of beliefs that can be or is universally known without the conversion of being incorporated within a specific community of people. In effect, it is to underwrite the Enlightenment assumption that we are most fully ourselves when we are free of all traditions and communities other than those we have chosen from the position of complete autonomy.[23] In such a context, suffering

---

22. Surin, *Theology and the Problem of Evil*, p. 23.
23. In *Whose Justice? Which Rationality?* (Notre Dame: University of Notre Dame Press, 1988), Alasdair MacIntyre says,

It was a central aspiration of the Enlightenment . . . to provide for debate in the public realm standards and methods of rational justification by which alternative courses of action in every sphere of life could be adjudged just or unjust, rational or irrational, enlightened or unenlightened. So, it was hoped, reason would displace authority and tradition. Rational justification was to appeal to principles undeniable by any rational person and therefore independent of all those social and cultural particularities which the Enlightenment thinkers took to be the mere accidental clothing of reason in particular times and places. And that rational justification could be nothing other than what the thinkers of the Enlightenment had said that it was came to be accepted, at least

cannot help but appear absurd, since it always stands as a threat to that autonomy.

Lest it be thought that I am being particularly hard on the epistemological assumptions of the Enlightenment, let me say that I think what the great Enlightenment thinkers often did was to provide a secular account of Christian tendencies.[24] To make this case, I will need to make

---

by the vast majority of educated people, in post-Enlightenment cultural and social orders. . . .

What the Enlightenment made us for the most part blind to and what we now need to recover is a conception of rational enquiry as embodied in a tradition, a conception according to which the standards of rational justification themselves emerge from and are part of a history in which they are vindicated by the way in which they transcend the limitations of and provide remedies for the defects of their predecessors within the history of that same tradition (pp. 6-7).

The constructive account I am trying to develop in this book obviously makes me sympathetic to the main outlines of MacIntyre's alternative to the Enlightenment.

24. I wrote this book prior to the publication of Charles Taylor's magisterial *Sources of the Self: The Making of the Modern Identity* (Cambridge: Harvard University Press, 1989). Taylor's book provides a substantial account to document this claim. Particularly significant for my subject is Taylor's account of modernity's transformation of the Puritans' discovery of the moral significance of "ordinary life." What began as an attempt to affirm that the fullness of Christians' existence could be found in the daily activities of their lives became—often under the impulse of an uncontrollable commitment to universal benevolence—an attempt to subject all of life to instrumental control. As Taylor notes, "The tremendous importance of the instrumental stance in modern culture is overdetermined. It represents the convergence of more than one stream. It is supported not just by the new science and not just by the dignity attaching to disengaged rational control; it has also been central to the ethics of ordinary life from its theological origins on. Affirming ordinary life has meant valuing the efficacious control of things by which it is

some unguarded generalizations as well as historical judgments that to be defended would require greater nuance than I offer here. However, it is my hope that such generalization will help us better understand our peculiar situation and the particular dilemma in which medicine finds itself.

Surin rightly criticizes modern theodicies that are built on foundational epistemologies in such a way that the problem of evil is at once conceived in an ahistorical manner and claimed solvable in equally ahistorical terms. Yet this approach, I suspect, reflects but the continuing habit of mind schooled by Christian pretensions that our beliefs are explanatory accounts sufficient to show why "the way things are" are such by necessity. I think this habit of mind developed when Christianity became a civilizational religion oriented to provide the ethos necessary to sustain an empire. Rather than being a set of convictions about God's work in Jesus Christ requiring conversion and membership in a community, Christianity became that set of beliefs which explains why the way things are is the way things were meant to be for any right-thinking person, converted or not.

There is a definite sociological correlative to this understanding of Christianity. It is the seeming correlative between the task of the church and the task of the state. Christians, who once had to try to survive and endure in often hostile political contexts, now have a stake in insuring that the policies of the Christian emperor will be successful. In order to do so, we must see history as a sphere of strict cause and effect, and thus exclude chance as much

---

preserved and enhanced as well as valuing the detachment from purely personal enjoyments which would blunt our dedication to its general flourishing" (p. 232). One can only wish that Taylor might have suggested how medicine became a character in this drama.

as possible from any explanatory account of history. In such a context, evil appears as that which has not yet come under our control. Crucial to this set of assumptions is the assumption that the good must ultimately triumph; otherwise the universe as well as the social order is incoherent. In such a context, the "problem of evil" is—to put it crudely but I think accurately—the challenge to show why those with the right beliefs do not always win in worldly terms. Theodicy in the theoretical mode, which is acutely criticized by Surin, is but the metaphysical expression of this deep-seated presumption that our belief in God is irrational if it does not put us on the winning side of history.

This explains the extraordinary presumption that a crisis of faith is created by "bad things happening to good people." Here a mechanistic metaphysic is combined with a sentimental account of God; in this way the pagan assumption that god or the gods are to be judged by how well it or they insure the successful outcome of human purposes is underwritten in the name of Christianity.[25] It is assumed

---

25. Hall's criticism of Kushner's *When Bad Things Happen to Good People* is extremely interesting in this respect. In *God and Human Suffering* he notes,

There is, strangely, a conspicuous absence of love in Kushner's discussion of God and human suffering. I say strangely because, unlike *some* of my fellow Christians, I do not accept the idea that love is an exclusively Christian attribute for the divine Being. The whole bent of Israel's theology is informed by the divine *agape* (*hesed*), and while this is undoubtedly more consistently associated with "righteousness" in the older (Judaic) tradition, it should never be reduced to "goodness." For Israel too, the divine love is beyond good and evil as these are regularly interpreted in the human sphere. It is not simply God's "goodness" that prevents God from executing the frequently entertained thought that it would be

that the attributes of such a god or gods can be known and characterized abstractly. But the God of Abraham, Isaac, and

> better, wiser, and more just simply to annul the already sullied covenant, perhaps to annihilate the wicked world! From beginning to end of this story told in the continuity of the Testaments, it is love, sheer love, that constitutes the basis (and the complicating factor!) of the relation between the principal characters.
>
> Because Kushner fails to grasp (or at least to express) this, his response to the fact of human suffering, while full of practical insights, is theologically and humanly unsatisfying. He ends, as do so many liberal Christians, with "religion" being pragmatically useful to sufferers, but it is the sufferer himself or herself who has to derive whatever meaning he or she can from the experience. Because the first (ontological!) principle is missing in this treatment, i.e., that "God is love," the second (soteriological) principle is also missing: grace. It becomes a matter of our wresting from our "bad" experiences whatever "good" we can get from them—of course "with God's help." (pp. 156-57)

Hall illustrates his point with several quotations from Kushner's book, including this one: "Let me suggest that the bad things that happen to us in our lives do not have a meaning when they happen to us. They do not happen for any good reason which would cause us to accept them willingly. But we can give them a meaning. We can redeem these tragedies from senselessness by imposing meaning on them" (*When Bad Things Happen to Good People* [New York: Schocken Books, 1981], p. 136). Of course, the telling word here is "impose," which presumes that we must make up for what God cannot supply. Hall offers this concluding comment:

> Kushner's treatment of the subject seems to me, then, to be a capitulation to modernity. It wants to retain the practical *results* of biblical faith without their ontological foundations. I believe that there are resources of wisdom in the ancient world of the Jews and the Christians which this author has not tapped. The *mythos* of the suffering God—of the God who yearns parentally towards creation; of the God who is not power*less* but whose power expresses itself unexpectedly in the weakness of love: this, I believe, is not only a more *profound* image of God than Kushner's limited

Jacob is not the god that creates something called the "problem of evil"; rather, that problem is created by a god about which the most important facts seem to be that it exists and is morally perfect as well as all-powerful—that is, the kind of god that emperors need to legitimate the "necessity" of their rule.

---

deity, it is also more accessible to the human spirit. For every one of us knows, if we've lived and loved at all, something of the meaning of *that* yearning, *that* weak power, *that* powerful weakness. (p. 158)

Although I find Hall's criticism of Kushner persuasive, I am not convinced that appeals to "God's suffering" can and should comfort the Don Wanderhopes. Indeed, as Hall's own, fuller account in his book makes clear, the affirmation of a "suffering God" must be placed within the ongoing narrative of God's redemption of creation through the cross and resurrection of Christ:

God's response to suffering is neither just a theory nor a story—"Once upon a time. . . ." Or, if it is a story, it is an unfinished story. The story, as Nicholas Lash says, "has, as yet, *no ending.*" The Christian propensity to give the story an ending—and a very happy one—may well be related to Christian reluctance to *participate in* the story, to tell it as if it were all over and done with, so that their "witness" had simply to be a verbal one—and even that, for the most part, without much of a struggle of soul or mind! The truth is that the story goes on. It is a tale of the continuing movement of God towards the world, of conquest from within. It involves in a central way a people, grasped by grace and compassion, searching out and identifying themselves with other people—especially with history's victims (Matthew 25). Not that this people possesses a special talent for compassion or vicarious suffering! Not that it alone, and under the nomenclature *church,* provides the "comfort" (Isaiah 40) that suffering humanity needs! Whatever capacity the church of Jesus Christ has for being a community of suffering, where the very sharing of the burden can constitute the beginning of the healing process, is a capacity which it is always itself receiving from beyond its own possibilities. It

Why *"Anthropodicy"* Has Replaced *Theodicy*

It is certainly true that the theoretical god of theoretical theodicies has made many concerned about the problem of suffering. Yet I think it is also the case that the attempt to defend such a god in the face of human suffering is largely irrelevant for the lives of most people actually doing the suffering. This is so because the god that such theodicies try to justify is, by definition, largely irrelevant to most people's lives. I am well aware that pollsters tell us that over 90 percent of the American people believe in god, but it is extremely unclear what such a claim means. I suspect that the god in which most of us believe, or at least the god with which we live our lives, is the god we find in theoretical theodicies, the god unable to call into existence a people who can provide an alternative to the world. The true god has been driven from the world—or at best has been made

---

is a case of the comforted comforting, the healed healing, the forgiven showing mercy.

The principle of grace, therefore, is strictly upheld. But what must not be upheld—what Christianity at the end of the Constantinian era must at last root out—is the kind of spectator spirituality which, having taken to itself in some domesticated form "the benefits of *his* passion," is itself able to exist in a suffering world without either passion or compassion. . . . The Christian faith's manner of addressing the multifold questions implied in the title of this work, "God and Human Suffering," will be assessed finally, not on the basis of the adequacy or inadequacy of its theology, but, like all things else, by its fruits, that is, on the basis of the church's deportment of *itself* in a suffering world. (pp. 141-42)

For the most complete treatment in modern theology of the theme of the suffering God, see Paul Fiddes, *The Creative Suffering of God* (New York: Oxford University Press, 1988).

a transcendent watchdog, a bureaucratic manager—by the assumption that we must control our existence by acquiring the power to eradicate from our lives anything that threatens our autonomy as individuals.[26]

Ernest Becker has been one of the most insightful commentators on the implications of this worldview, which he characterizes as a product of the Newtonian revolution. According to Becker, it was Newton's great achievement to rehabilitate nature as having human significance—that is, to show that a nature which is not animated with godly purpose can nonetheless serve human ends. But this rehabilitation came at a cost, as Becker explains:

> If the new nature was so regular and beautiful, then why was there evil in the world? Man needed a new theodicy, but this time he could not put the burden on God. Something entirely different had to be done to explain evil in the world, a theodicy without Divine intervention. The new theodicy had to be a natural one, a "secular" one. The challenge was all the greater because the human mind was not prepared for such ingenuity: the idea of a "secular" theodicy was a contradiction in words and in emotions. Yet it describes exactly what was needed: an "anthropodicy." Evil had to be explained as existing in the world apart from God's intention or justification. Furthermore, as God was gradually eliminated from science as an explanatory principle, the need for a complete theodicy also finally vanished. There could be no sensible explanation for *all* the evil to which life is subject, apart from

---

26. Given this state of affairs, believer and nonbeliever alike are put in a strange situation. When confronted with the suffering of a child, believers often discover that, despite their explicit convictions, they are in fact practical atheists; unbelievers sometimes discover that, despite their explicit disbelief, they are sustained by the habits of a community of belief—thus the strange life of a Don Wanderhope.

a belief in God—certainly no explanation that mere mortals could attain. Consequently, man had to settle for a new *limited* explanation, an anthropodicy which would cover only *those evils that allow for human remedy.* The only way to achieve this new explanation was gradually to shift the burden from reliance on God's will to the belief in man's understanding and powers. This was a shift that was to occupy the whole Enlightenment, and it was not easily accomplished. In fact, it is still not accomplished today.[27]

If Becker is right—if the real problem is how to account for those evils that allow for human intervention—we

---

27. Becker, *The Structure of Evil* (New York: George Braziller, 1968), p. 18. Of course, this insight is not unique to Becker; it has also come from others such as Camus. For example, Richard Bauckman, in discussing Camus's assessment of Dostoyevsky's *The Brothers Karamazov,* notes that Camus saw that Ivan's revolt against God for the cruel and meaningless destruction of children (in Book V, Chapter 4) encapsulates the history of the modern age in which theodicy has been replaced by anthropodicy:

In the ancient regime, the God of theodicy served to sanction the injustices of society, justifying suffering by means of his eschatological purpose. This God had to be rejected in the modern revolt against the injustices of this world. But the rebel who wishes to replace that world by a new just world must himself replace God. Humanity—or at least the political elite, who know there is no God—must take control of human destiny in order to replace the unjust world of the dead God with its own new world of human justice. But in order to subject history to this purpose, the revolutionary elite justifies any means. Innocent suffering may be inflicted for the sake of future justice, and so the tyranny of the revolutionary regime silences revolt just as effectively as God did in the tyranny of the old divine right monarchies. For an eschatological theodicy which justified suffering, the modern age has substituted an eschatological anthropology which also justifies suffering. Thus Camus's interpretation of Ivan throws important light on the problem of theodicy in our age. How can Ivan's protest

can better understand why illness and, correlatively, medicine seem to become the context for raising the question of evil. As moderns we are bothered by the evil effects of hurricanes, tornadoes, and volcanoes, but they do not trouble us the way sickness does. If we are injured in a natural disaster or, perhaps, an automobile accident, we think that is bad luck. Such evil really requires no general explanation, since there is nothing we can do or could have done to prevent it. Once we no longer believe in the God of creation, there is no god that such disasters call into question.

But sickness is quite another matter. Sickness should not exist because we think of it as something in which we can intervene and which we can ultimately eliminate. Sickness challenges our most cherished presumption that we are or at least can be in control of our existence. Sickness creates the problem of "anthropodicy" because it challenges our most precious and profound belief that humanity has in fact become god. Against the backdrop of such a belief, we conclude that sickness should not exist.

In such a context, medicine becomes the mirror image of theoretical theodicies sponsored by the Enlightenment because it attempts to save our profoundest hopes that sickness should and can be eliminated. We must assume a strict causal order so that this new emperor can be assured of success. We do not need a community capable of caring for the ill; all we need is an instrumental rationality made powerful by technological sophistication.[28]

---

be maintained and not lapse into the cynical terror of the Grand Inquisitor? (From "Theodicy from Ivan Karamazov to Moltmann," *Modern Theology* 4 [Oct. 1987]: 86).

28. Thus Bryan Turner argues, "To regard illness as a text open to a variety of perspectives is a radical approach to sickness, because it

The ideology that is institutionalized in medicine requires that we interpret all illness as pointless. By "pointless" I mean that it can play no role in helping us live our lives well. Illness is an absurdity in a history formed by the commitment to overcome all evils that potentially we can control. I suspect that this is one of the reasons we have so much difficulty dealing with chronic illness—it should not exist but it does. It would almost be better to eliminate the subjects of such illness rather than to have them remind us that our project to eliminate illness has made little progress.

It is only against this background that we can appreciate the widespread assumption that what we *can* do through the office of science and medicine we *ought* to do. Whereas it used to be a physician's first obligation *not* to act, we now believe our commitment to the abolition of limits makes the physician's first obligation *to act* through the office of medicine. As a result, physicians lose their freedom to care for the sick because they are now judged by

points to some of the problems in the medical model which underlies the basis of institutionalized, scientific, technologically directed medicine. As we have seen, the medical model as the principal paradigm of modern medicine is derived from the postivistic philosophy of Descartes, who established an unbridgeable gap between the life of the mind and that of the body. Modern medicine, treating the body as a sort of machine, regards illness and disease as malfunctions of the body's mechanics. All 'real' diseases have specific causal mechanisms which can be ultimately identified and treated. Such an approach rules out the centrality and importance of experience, feeling, emotion and interpretation in the phenomenology of sickness and disease. A classic illustration of the medical model is germ theory, derived from the scientific medical work of Pasteur and Koch in the nineteenth century; their work established a scientific basis for the emergence of medicine as a profession equipped with a satisfactory knowledge basis" (*Medical Power and Social Knowledge* [London: Sage Publications, 1987], pp. 213-14).

the predictability of their performance; physicians must now provide a "cure" based on the assumption that what is "wrong" with the sick can be traced to specific "causes." The patient becomes the consumer, and thus "the old conception of medicine as a collaborative enterprise, in which doctor and patient each have freedoms and responsibilities, can no longer be sustained."[29]

One of the most disturbing aspects of this change is the assumption that a medicine so formed needs no justification. We assume that we ought to do what we can do because such is the way of compassion. But as Oliver O'Donovan reminds us in *Begotten or Made?* compassion is hardly a virtue that can stand by itself. "Compassion is the virtue of being moved to action by the sight of suffering— that is to say, by the infringement of passive freedoms. It is a virtue that circumvents thought, since it prompts us immediately to action. It is a virtue that presupposes that an answer has already been found to the question 'What needs to be done?' "[30] When compassion becomes the overriding virtue in a world in which we believe that human inventiveness has no limits, the result can only be the increasing subjection of our lives to a technology grown cruel by its Promethean pretensions. Thus, ironically, the evil we now suffer is the result of our fevered attempts to avoid the reality that we will always live in a world where some children will die. In an attempt to "solve the problem of evil," we cannot help but suffer from the results of failing to recognize that it cannot be solved if by "solved" we mean "eliminated."

---

29. Oliver O'Donovan, *Begotten or Made?* (Oxford: Clarendon Press, 1984), pp. 1-10.

30. O'Donovan, *Begotten or Made?* p. 11.

Why We Still Cannot Avoid the Suffering of Children

E ven if I have successfully convinced you that it is a mistake to try to "solve" the problem of evil, particularly in our circumstances, we still confront children who are suffering and possibly dying. I have no answer to the question of why children suffer because I do not want to grant the presuppositions that often give rise to such a question. I do, however, have a suggestion about why we are especially bothered by the suffering of children.

When illness breaks into our lives, it subverts our plans and projects. As adults we may respond more or less well to our illness, but at least the illness seems to have a context— we can make it part of our ongoing story. Indeed, it may well be that one of the most valuable functions of medicine is to help us go on in the face of an illness that may not finally be curable.

In the preface of his whimsically titled book, *The Man Who Mistook His Wife for a Hat,* Oliver Sacks stresses the importance of making a case history a personal story:

> Animals get diseases, but only man falls radically into sickness.
>
> My work, my life, is all with the sick—but the sick and their sickness drives me to thoughts which, perhaps, I might otherwise not have. So much so that I am compelled to ask, with Nietzsche: "As for sickness: are we not almost tempted to ask whether we could get along without it?"—and to see the questions it raises as fundamental in nature. Constantly my patients drive me to question, and constantly my questions drive me to patients—thus in the stories or studies which follow there is a continual movement from one to the other.
>
> Studies, yes; why stories, or cases? Hippocrates intro-

duced the historical conception of disease, the idea that diseases have a course, from their first intimations to their climax or crisis, and thence to their happy or fatal resolution. Hippocrates thus introduced the case history, a description, or depiction, of the natural history of disease—precisely expressed by the old word "pathography." Such histories are a form of natural history—but they tell us nothing about the individual and *his* history; they convey nothing of the person, and the experience of the person, as he faces, and struggles to survive, his disease. There is no "subject" in a narrow case history; modern case histories allude to the subject in a cursory phrase ("a trisomic albino female of 21"), which could as well apply to a rat as a human being. To restore the human subject at the centre—the suffering, afflicted, fighting, human subject—we must deepen a case history to a narrative or tale; only then do we have a "who" as well as a "what," a real person, a patient, in relation to disease—in relation to the physical.[31]

Ironically, with the instrumentalization of modern medicine, the patient is seen as a passive recipient of medical expertise, and he or she can no longer be seen as a person with a life story. "Yet it is only within a life story," notes David Barnard, "that illness has a meaningful place. And to see the patient's illness as a development in a biography— rather than as an isolated series of biological events—is precisely to recover a context of meaning for medical interventions. Within that context, it is possible to appreciate both the patient's own values and hopes, which supply a framework for evaluating specific medical interventions, and his or her reservoirs of agency and strength, which are nec-

---

31. Sacks, *The Man Who Mistook His Wife for a Hat and Other Clinical Tales* (New York: Harper & Row, 1985), pp. xiii-xiv.

essary complements to physician power in healing relationships."[32]

I think childhood suffering bothers us so deeply because we assume that children lack a life story which potentially gives their illness some meaning. In that respect I
suspect we often fail to appreciate the richness of their young
world as well as their toughness and resilience. But I suspect
that what bothers us even more about childhood suffering
is that it makes us face our deepest suspicions that all of us
lack a life story which would make us capable of responding
to illness in a manner that would enable us to go on as
individuals, as friends, as parents, and as a community. I
suspect that if Christian convictions have any guidance to
give us about how we are to understand as well as respond
to suffering, it is by helping us discover that our lives are
located in God's narrative—the God who has not abandoned
us even when we or someone we care deeply about is ill.
The development of these suggestions, however, will have
to wait till the next chapter.

God and Human Suffering

Nothing I have said up to this point is meant to deflect
the agony of or make less challenging the suffering
and death of a child. Neither do I wish to imply that
Auschwitz and Hiroshima can be "explained" away. Obviously suffering, seemingly unnecessary and pointless
suffering, grips our lives in a manner that rightly leaves us

---

32. David Barnard, "Religion and Medicine: A Meditation on
Lines of A. J. Heschel," *Soundings* 63 (Winter 1985): 456-57.

numb. My point is not to deny the reality of suffering—in particular, suffering that bears the mark of evil (that is, suffering which seems "caused" by a power for no reason)—but rather to suggest that there is no such thing as suffering that challenges belief in the existence of God as such.

Just as "God" is not a concept with a univocal meaning but rather the name Christians have been given for the One who alone is worthy to be worshiped, so "suffering" is not simply a "given" but comes in great variety and with different significance correlative to the narratives of our particular lives. Bryan Turner gets at this point in *Religion and Social Theory:* "Although not denying the universality of the facts of sexual reproduction and death, social differences deeply influence our unique experience of sexuality and finitude, and our location in the social structure closely impinges upon our common religious experiences of the body. Starting with the problem of the fragility of the body and the inevitability of death, it is important to note that death has a social history and that the biology of death is also a socially constructed event."[33]

It is reasonable to think that this surely must be wrong. Many would argue that while there is great variety in the ways in which people marry and bury, that variety in and of itself does not deny that there is a fundamental experience of suffering and death which we all must have in common. For example, recoiling at the innocent suffering and death of children seems to be a response all people share. Although it takes different forms, the mourning of a parent for his or her child seems to evoke in each of us a sympathy sufficient to establish the existence of a common experience. Moreover,

---

33. Turner, *Religion and Social Theory: A Materialist Perspective* (New Jersey: Humanities Press, 1983), p. 228.

it is equally true that, because we see ourselves united by such common suffering, we feel compelled to look for ways to eliminate the causes of that suffering.

Even though these sentiments are widely and strongly held, it is simply not the case that all people everywhere respond to the suffering of children with the same outrage or even perceive what the children endure as suffering. Take, for example, Colin Turnbull's book entitled *The Mountain People.* Turnbull describes how the Ik would "watch a child with eager anticipation as it crawled toward the fire, then burst into gay and happy laughter as it plunged a skinny hand into the coals. Such times were the few times when parental affection showed itself; a mother would glow with pleasure to hear such joy occasioned by her offspring, and pull it tenderly out of the fire."[34]

Turnbull later describes the pleasure he felt at being awakened one night by the mournful wailing one normally associates with grief over a death. He thought this might actually be an Ik mother crying over the death of her child. The crying, it turned out, did involve the death of a son, but it was not a cry of despair. Rather, the child's mother and father had argued about whether the child should be buried immediately or the next morning. If they waited, the burial would involve a funeral that would require the parents to feast the mourners. Wanting to avoid this, the husband had tried to force his wife to dig the hole for the grave during the night, and when she refused, he beat her—thus her screams.[35]

It may well be thought that this is an unfair example.

------

34. Turnbull, *The Mountain People* (New York: Torchbooks, 1972), p. 112.
35. Turnbull, *The Mountain People,* pp. 129-30.

The Ik, after all, were a tribe whose life had been fundamentally distorted by relocation, so they may not have been acting "normally." Moreover, there is always the possibility that Turnbull's anthropological presuppositions biased his account. Yet we do not have to go as far as Africa to find people who do not share Don Wanderhope's concern over a suffering child. Take, for instance, the article entitled "Many AIDS Children Orphaned, Abandoned at Birth," which appeared in the *Durham Morning Herald* a few years ago. It stated that about one-third of the children born with AIDS are abandoned at birth.[36] It may well be the case that some parents abandon their AIDS-afflicted children because they care so deeply that they cannot stand to watch these infants suffer and die, but it is surely the case that many of these parents abandon their offspring because they mistakenly fear they might contract the disease by caring for these children. Even among enlightened and humane people—perhaps especially among them—the fear of death can qualify what we normally assume are our overriding commitments to our children.

But, some might argue, even if some people do not care for their children in a way we think is "natural," we can still think they ought to do so. Thus parents who abandon their AIDS-afflicted children should not do so; thus the Ik ought to be the kind of people who see that a child who burns itself is in pain and that this is sufficient reason to protect a child from dangers like fire. Even though I am in complete agreement with these observations, they are nonetheless reminders that our perception of pain and suffering as well as the significance that we ascribe to them is correlative to ways of life that are not simply given but depend on a community's habits of care. In this case our attitude

---

36. *Durham Morning Herald*, 4 Sept. 1987, p. 18A.

about the suffering and death of children obviously draws on presuppositions about the significance of children that are not universally shared.

For example, in discussing *The Blood of the Lamb,* I noted that Don Wanderhope was not as crushed by the deaths of Rena, his girlfriend, and Greta, his wife, as he was by the death of Carol, his daughter. In his narrative he pointed out that shortly after Rena's death, he was distracted by his father's illness. And after Greta's death he mentioned that she seemed to have had a self-destructive streak that made her suicide almost inevitable. Yet these factors still do not explain why Wanderhope should see Carol's suffering and death as such a singular challenge, in a way he did not see the deaths of Rena and Greta.

Wanderhope's attitude in this regard does not seem unusual—in fact, it is an example of a widespread attitude in our culture. Suffering comes in all shapes and sizes. We are all going to die, some of us in an untimely and even horrible fashion. So why does the suffering and death of children seem to shake us to the roots in a way that other forms of suffering and death do not? It may be, of course, that some of us are equally bothered by other things—the horror of slaughter in war or the destruction of the Jews in the Holocaust. But for many of us the challenge of suffering confronts us most compellingly in the death of a child.

It is particularly interesting to consider this issue in relation to illness and medical care. I suspect that what bothers us about illness is not simply the pain and suffering it occasions but the absurdity of it. There is simply no reason why I should have Parkinson's disease. It is almost comforting if I am able to see my disease as a consequence of my lifestyle, because that at least helps make sense of my suffering. The fact that I have lung cancer because I have always smoked does not make my illness any less painful, but at least I know *why* I have what I have.

I suspect that this attitude lies behind some of the unspoken presumptions surrounding the AIDS crisis. It is not simply that some people believe that homosexuals, because of their alleged immorality, get what they deserve when they acquire AIDS; more than that, the association of AIDS with homosexuality provides a framework that makes the very existence of AIDS explicable. It is admittedly strange to think it comforting to know that the lifestyle associated with modernity helps account for the rates of certain illnesses—that bad diets and stress and heavy smoking often figure in the frequent occurrence of heart disease and cancer—but in fact without this knowledge such illnesses seem even more frightening. Our being able to associate our illnesses, at both a social and a personal level, with a causal system gives us a sense of control that seems to make their destructive outcomes less terrible.

But that is exactly what it seems we cannot do in the case of ill children. No doubt some children are sick because of the actions of adults—fetal problems can be caused by a mother's smoking or drinking or taking drugs during pregnancy, and some children suffer the effects of lead poisoning and pollution—but the fact that children suffer and even die from such causes makes their deaths no less tragic. Most childhood illnesses, however, cannot be blamed on anyone or any system. It just happened that Carol Wanderhope contracted leukemia. It just happens that some children are born with Down's syndrome. The sick child simply gets the bad luck of the draw. There is no "causal" explanation that can remove the absurdity of a child's suffering and death.

In this respect it is quite interesting to note how the suffering of a child can be mapped in terms of attempts to understand or explain the existence of suffering and evil. For example, one of the most common responses to the "problem of evil" is the free-will defense. Evil and suffering exist, it is said, because of a misuse of creaturely freedom. God willed that we be creatures who would serve God out of choice, but as such we can also use our freedom to reject God's authority. God could not create us as free beings who would always use our freedom to do good, for if God did so then our actions would be determined. Thus Richard Rice argues, "If we ask why God created a world in which suffering was even possible, the answer is because the highest values of which we know, such as love, loyalty, and compassion, presuppose personal freedom. God cannot create a world where personal values are possible without giving its inhabitants the freedom such values presuppose. All this means there was a risk in creating beings morally free. There was the genuine possibility that they would fall, and this is where evil began. God's creatures, then, are responsible for evil and its consequences, while God is blameless. Because it began in an act of personal freedom, there is no explanation for evil. Indeed evil makes no sense at all."[37]

The free-will defense may help us "explain" much of the suffering around us—suffering from war, poverty, and famine, for example. But if we think it can "explain" the suffering of Carol Wanderhope, then we are surely asking such a defense to do more than it is capable of doing. Even if one assumes rather physicalist accounts of the inheritance of "original sin," it still does not follow that Carol Wanderhope "deserved" leukemia; nor does it comfort us to believe that leukemia is the result of humankind's sinfulness and thus denotes the general disruption of God's good order.

---

37. Rice, "The Mystery of Suffering," *Update* 2 (Oct. 1986): 3.

That may be, and it may help explain our general disorder, but it does nothing to explain the particularity of Carol Wanderhope's illness.

To be sure, more powerful and compelling accounts can be given, but I think they are no more successful at explaining the Carol Wanderhopes. Take, for example, the account that Douglas John Hall offers in *God and Human Suffering.* He notes that the story Christians tell about creation presupposes that struggle belongs to the created order, which makes suffering intrinsic to our existence. Adam was created alone so that he could discover in the midst of the goodness of creation that it is not good to be alone. Without the capacity for this recognition, how could we ever learn the joy of human fellowship?[38]

Our suffering also derives from our necessary experience of limits. There is much we cannot do, as Hall points out— "we are not big enough or strong enough or wise enough, old enough or young enough, agile enough, versatile enough." But without limits we would not know the meaning of being "creature." Indeed, those very limits, as well as our loneliness, create the condition that makes another very "creaturely" limit possible: temptation. As Hall suggests, "The serpent, a creature of God (for there is no *ultimate* dualism here), makes certain that the human beings become conscious of the thought that they might employ their wits and *exceed* the limits of their creaturehood. How much of the suffering that belongs to our personal and collective life is the consequence of reaching beyond our potentiality—of seeking to become gods? . . . Yet this temptation appears to be given with creaturehood as such; one cannot avoid concluding that temptation, according to this tradition, is

---

38. Hall, *God and Human Suffering,* pp. 53-62.

an aspect of what 'should be.' The tempter cannot easily be separated from the Creator."[39]

Finally, Hall notes that as creatures we are created anxious—what will tomorrow bring? who can we trust? Our anxiety, which is the source of our creativity as well as our sin, is intrinsic to our being as creatures; sin is not. That is, sin is not innate in us as creatures, just as the Fall was not inherent in the original creation, yet the potentiality for sin could not be excluded if we were to be rather than not be. Without anxiety we could never achieve "any real depth of being," according to Hall:

> Only a chatty cheerfulness could result from a humanity in which no anxiety were present. We do not have to speculate about this, for all around us today we can encounter persons who for the sake of achieving peace of mind have effected, with or without the help of medical or pharmaceutical technology, an ersatz freedom from anxiety. But they have purchased this alleged freedom at a very high price: the price of authenticity and depth, the price of passion and of feeling. . . .
>
> What we are admitting, surely, in such reflections as these, is that life without any kind of suffering would be no life at all; it would be a form of death. Life—the life of the spirit like the life of the body—depends in some mysterious way upon *the struggle to be.* This presupposes, as the condition necessary to life itself, the presence of life's antithesis, that is, of that which threatens or negates, circumscribes or challenges.[40]

All of this means that death must be part of God's good creation. What sin brought was not mere physical death but

---

39. Hall, *God and Human Suffering*, p. 55.
40. Hall, *God and Human Suffering*, pp. 59-60. Hall's account ob-

a kind of death that threatens absolute aloneness, a threat that humankind works against in positive ways. "While death is the enemy," Hall says, "it is also a useful, perhaps even a necessary enemy. In this [the Christian] tradition, even death must be God's servant, serving God's project, namely, the blossoming of the *life* of the world. With its limiting and its questioning of every supposed security, death introduces a dimension of profundity into our life which could probably never be apart from it. . . . As Martin Heidegger has insisted, it is because we are being-towards-death that we are capable of a *compassion . . .* towards one another, i.e., of a sympathy (suffering-with) that transcends mere passion."[41]

---

viously owes much to Tillich as well as to Reinhold Niebuhr. Inasmuch as he draws on Tillich and Niebuhr, however, Hall fails to see how their accounts of the "human condition" assume exactly the kind of "universality" that denies our historicity. Put in terms made popular by George Lindbeck in his *Nature of Doctrine: Religion and Theology in a Postliberal Age* (Philadelphia: Westminster Press, 1984), Tillich and Niebuhr are classic examples of experiential-expressivist theologians who attempt to show that Christian convictions, properly understood, are but provocative accounts of the human condition qua human condition. In that sense, Tillich and Niebuhr (and, I think, Hall) remain classical liberal theologians. If I tried to display my own dissatisfaction with this account of sin, as well as with Hall's account of theological language, it would simply distract from the general theme of this book. Suffice it to say that I do not believe that sin is a universal condition of humans qua humans. I believe that all of creation has been disordered by sin. Yet to acknowledge our sinfulness is a theological achievement that requires much training via being formed by a truthful community. Indeed, I suspect that the kind of account that Tillich, Niebuhr, and Hall provide is intelligible because they presuppose the existence of such a community and a corresponding narrative. For a fuller account of these matters, see my book entitled *After Christendom: Christians Living in Awkward Times* (forthcoming).

41. Hall, *God and Human Suffering*, p. 61.

There is obviously much wisdom in Hall's account of our creaturely existence. His analysis helps us see that we rightly distinguish between suffering that is evil or unnecessary (which we should try to eliminate) and that which is not.[42] Moreover, given this account of suffering, we better understand why the cry of pain is absolutely necessary to our being able to identify and respond to injustice and sin. Yet all this still does not and should not explain the suffering and death of Carol Wanderhope. We may think that Don Wanderhope may have grown more compassionate and wise because of the illness and death of his daughter, but it is quite another matter to say that her illness and death were

---

42. While this distinction is clear in principle, we will see that it is by no means easy to make in practice. For example, in their book entitled *AIDS and the Church* (Philadelphia: Westminster, 1982), Earl Shelp and Ron Sunderland note that "the New Testament recognizes suffering as a part of daily living that must be accepted and endured with fortitude. The troubles to be borne in this earthly existence are of little consequence compared to the life that is 'hidden with Christ in God' (Col. 3:3). The New Testament, however, addresses sufferings at three levels. First, some afflictions clearly were the consequences of imprisonment and persecution because of the believer's witness to faith in Jesus Christ as Lord. Thus was Stephen stoned to death. Second, suffering may be the result of oppression by one person or group of another person or group. The most frequently cited biblical example is the oppression of the weak and helpless by the wealthy and powerful. Third, pain and suffering may be due to disease or physical or mental disability" (p. 56). Using these distinctions and drawing on Jesus' healing ministry, Shelp and Sunderland argue that the latter form of suffering is properly the occasion for compassion as well as an attempt to overcome that which is the cause of the suffering. While I do not disagree with them in principle, I think the matter is more complex than they acknowledge, since it is no simple matter to distinguish "suffering that is part of our daily living" from suffering which comes as part of our discipleship.

meant to make him more compassionate or to help him discover "how long is the mourners' bench upon which we sit." We may even believe that the deaths of others who were important to Wanderhope—those of his brother, his girl-friend, his father, and his wife—helped make him the compassionate father he obviously was. Although it would be a good thing if Wanderhope were so schooled by their deaths, they were not meant for such development, nor were they necessary for it.

In short, the problem with all free-will defenses of suffering (and even provocative accounts like Hall's are but forms of the free-will defense) is that they "explain" too much. What we must admit when we are confronted with the suffering and death of a Carol Wanderhope is that there is no "explanation." Rather, we rightly see and feel that such suffering has "no point." Good may come from such suffer-ing, and it may encourage us all the more to find a cure for leukemia, but it cannot thereby be explained or justified. It just happened.

However, the kind of account provided by Hall does help us notice important elements of our understanding of God's relation to human suffering that are often ignored in many free-will defenses. For Hall does not try, as Rice does, to absolve God. Rather, he in effect tells a story that places our existence in an ongoing history which provides us with skills of discrimination so that we are able to distinguish suffering that is evil from that which is explicable given our projects. The problem of evil is not about rectifying our suffering with some general notion of God's nature as all-powerful and good; rather, it is about what we mean by God's goodness itself, which for Christians must be con-strued in terms of God as the Creator who has called into existence a people called Israel so that the world might know that God has not abandoned us. There is no problem of suffering in general; rather, the question of suffering can be raised only in the context of a God who creates to redeem.

In this respect there is an odd conceptual connection between our being as creatures and our suffering. Creation did not have to be; it is God's free self-giving. That is why we can never show the necessary existence of God on the basis of creation, since such a demonstration would require that God could not have done otherwise than create. While it is certainly true that, having created, God would not be other than the God who creates, this does not provide us with an account of the God who would metaphysically require God to so create. Therefore, since the world exists contingently, there is no way to construe creation and God's relation to it other than by a narrative. Of course, that is what Hall is doing by suggesting that "suffering belongs to the order of creation insofar as struggle is necessary to the human glory that is God's intention for us."[43] For just as there is "no point" to God's creation, so there is "no point" to our suffering. Neither is finally subject to "explanation," and yet both remind us that our existence makes sense only insofar as we are able to place it in a narrative.

Because Christians—and, I might add, the community over time that gave us the Hebrew Scriptures—do not think they have a stake in God's being "blameless," to use Rice's word, they see no reason to refrain from expressing their pain. As Walter Brueggemann makes clear in his exposition of the Psalms, not only did Israel think it legitimate to complain, but she also developed an entire genre for lament.[44] Consider, for example, Psalm 13 (here taken from the RSV):

---

43. Hall, *God and Human Suffering,* p. 62.
44. Brueggemann, *The Message of the Psalms,* pp. 51-121. Moreover,

How long, O Lord? Wilt thou forget me for ever?
How long wilt thou hide thy face from me?
How long must I bear pain in my soul,
and have sorrow in my heart all the day?
How long shall my enemy be exalted over me?

Consider and answer me, O Lord my God;
lighten my eyes, lest I sleep the sleep of death;
lest my enemy say, "I have prevailed over him";
lest my foes rejoice because I am shaken.

But I have trusted in thy steadfast love;
my heart shall rejoice in thy salvation.
I will sing to the Lord, because he has dealt bountifully
     with me.

Brueggemann calls psalms of this kind psalms of disorientation because they challenge the assumption that our life is ordered and that an equilibrium has been established. These psalms do not try to hide the fact that things have not gone the way Israel thought they should have for her, for those who believe themselves to be the chosen people of God. As Brueggemann points out, Psalm 13 does end with an affirmation that the disorientation has been overcome, but many of the lament psalms do not end with anything like a resolution (e.g., Psalm 35, Psalm 86). Even in psalms like Psalm 13 the affirmation in the last verses does not suggest that the previous suffering is thereby made irrelevant. Rather, the suffering is simply acknowledged for what it is with no explanation given for it.

Rowan Crews rightly reminds us that the lament takes place in worship. The Psalms are formed by and form our praise of God ("The Praise of God and the Problem of Evil: A Doxological Approach to the Problem of Evil and Suffering," Ph.D. diss., Duke University, 1989).

Brueggemann notes that it is curious that the church, although finding itself "in a world increasingly experienced as disoriented," continues to use psalms of orientation, psalms that reassure us that God's creation is in good order. That may be a wonderful form of prophetic affirmation in such a world, but it may also reflect a self-deceptive optimism that is not based on the kind of hope made possible by our belief in God. This is what Brueggemann suspects:

> Such a denial and cover-up, which I take it to be, is an odd inclination for passionate Bible users, given the large number of psalms that are songs of lament, protest, and complaint about the incoherence that is experienced in the world. At least it is clear that a church that goes on singing "happy songs" in the face of raw reality is doing something very different from what the Bible itself does.
>
> I think that serious religious use of the lament psalms has been minimal because we have believed that faith does not mean to acknowledge and embrace negativity. We have thought that acknowledgment of negativity was somehow an act of unfaith, as though the very speech about it conceded too much about God's "loss of control."
>
> The point to be urged here is this: The use of these "psalms of darkness" may be judged by the world to be *acts of unfaith and failure,* but for the trusting community, their use is *an act of bold faith,* albeit a transformed faith. It is an act of bold faith on the one hand, because it insists that the world must be experienced as it really is and not in some pretended way. On the other hand, it is bold because it insists that all such experiences of disorder are a proper subject for discourse with God. There is nothing out of bounds, nothing precluded or inappropriate. Everything properly belongs in this conversation of the heart. To withhold parts of life from that conversation is in fact to

withhold part of life from the sovereignty of God. Thus these psalms make the important connection: everything must be *brought to speech,* and everything brought to speech must be *addressed to God,* who is the final reference for all of life.[45]

The psalms of lament do not simply reflect our experience; they are meant to form our experience of despair. They are meant to name the silences that our suffering has created. They bring us into communion with God and one another, communion that makes it possible to acknowledge our pain and suffering, to rage that we see no point to it, and yet our very acknowledgment of that fact makes us a people capable of living life faithfully. We are able to do so because we know that the God who has made our life possible is not a God merely of goodness and power, but the God whom we find manifested in the calling of Israel and the life, cross, and resurrection of Jesus of Nazareth. The God who calls us to service through worship is not a God who insures that our lives will not be disturbed; indeed, if we are faithful, we had better expect to experience a great deal of unrest. This may not be the God we want, but at least it is a God whose very complexity is so fascinating that our attention is captivated by the wonder of the life God has given us—a life that includes pain and suffering that seem to have no point.

We are encouraged to express our pain and suffering not simply because that provides a "healthy release." Once we understand how expressing pain and suffering can delegitimate theodicies meant to legitimate the status quo, then we can see that our willingness to expose our pain is

---

45. Brueggemann, *The Message of the Psalms,* pp. 51-52.

the means God gives us to help us identify and respond to evil and injustice. For creation is not as it ought to be. The lament is the cry of protest schooled by our faith in a God who would have us serve the world by exposing its false comforts and deceptions. From such a perspective one of the profoundest forms of faithlessness is the unwillingness to acknowledge our inexplicable suffering and pain.

Brueggemann observes that once we see the problem of pain and suffering from this perspective, we can better understand why the church has avoided using the psalms of lament:

> They lead us into dangerous acknowledgment of how life really is. They lead us into the presence of God where everything is not polite and civil. They cause us to think unthinkable thoughts and utter unutterable words. Perhaps worst, they lead us away from the comfortable religious claims of "modernity" in which everything is managed and controlled. In our modern experience, but probably also in every successful and affluent culture, it is believed that enough power and knowledge can tame the terror and eliminate the darkness. But our honest experience, both personal and public, attests to the resilience of the darkness, in spite of us. The remarkable thing about Israel is that it did not banish or deny the darkness from its religious enterprise. It embraces the darkness as the very stuff of new life. Indeed, Israel seems to know that new life comes [from] nowhere else.[46]

So Wanderhope's anguished "No!" in front of St. Jude was perhaps his most determinative act of faith. In that "no" he joined that great host of the faithful who believed that

---

46. Brueggemann, *The Message of the Psalms*, p. 53.

the God they worshiped is not a God who needs protection from our cries of pain and suffering. Ironically, the act of unbelief turns out to be committed by those who refuse to address God in their pain, thinking that God just might not be up to such confrontation.

Suffering Service

It may well be thought that the account I have given is nothing short of blasphemy. Are not Christians suppposed to see their suffering serving some good end for the life of faith? Earlier, for example, I cited Romans 5, where Paul says, "Therefore, since we are justified by faith, we have peace with God through our Lord Jesus Christ. Through him we have obtained access to this grace in which we stand, and we rejoice in our hope of sharing the glory of God. More than that, we rejoice in our sufferings, knowing that suffering produces endurance, and endurance produces character, and character produces hope, and hope does not disappoint us, because God's love has been poured into our hearts through the Holy Spirit which has been given to us" (vv. 1-5, RSV). We are to "rejoice in our sufferings."

This seems to indicate that for the early Christians suffering was but an opportunity for living in a way more faithful to the new age which they believed had begun in Christ. Their suffering did not make them question their belief in God, much less God's goodness; their suffering only confirmed their belief that they were part of Christ's church through baptism into his death. Their faith gave them a way to go on in the face of specific persecution and general misfortune. Suffering, even their suffering from evil and injustice, did not create a metaphysical problem needing solution; rather, it was a practical challenge requiring a communal response.

Any truthful account of the Christian life cannot exclude suffering as integral to that life. Yet it is important that this not become an invitation to make suffering an end in itself or to acquiesce to kinds of suffering that can and should be alleviated. Admittedly, this is not an easy distinction to make in theory or in practice, but it is the kind of distinction that must be hammered out by the common wisdom of a people who worship the God found on the cross of Jesus of Nazareth.

For example, it is important that we be able to distinguish those forms of suffering that derive directly from the way of life occasioned by our faithfulness to the cross from those forms of suffering that do not. The suffering to which Paul refers in Romans is the suffering that those who followed Jesus were to expect—social ostracism, persecution, unjust jailings, even martyrdom. Because they followed a savior who challenged religious, political, and economic authorities, they had to expect those same authorities to subject them to the same punishment to which they subjected him.[47] Christians are not to seek persecution as if such persecution would confirm their righteousness, but neither are they to be disconcerted if they are so persecuted.

The suffering that is a consequence of our living a faithful life has a different valence than that which is not. It certainly is not less painful, but at least we can understand why it is happening. This kind of suffering takes place

---

47. E. S. Gerstenberger and W. Schrage provide an excellent discussion of this point on pp. 164-87 in their book entitled *Suffering,* trans. John E. Steely (Nashville: Abingdon, 1977).

within a history that gives it a telos. In this respect this kind of suffering is not unlike the suffering that is a consequence of choosing any way of life which forces us to accept losses in the interest of securing what we perceive as a greater good. This kind of suffering is named from the beginning because we have a sense of why it is happening. Even the most extreme example of such suffering—parents confronting the horror of their children dying for their religious convictions—still seems to have a purpose; it is humanly possible for us to comprehend that horror. Yet for a child to die of disease seems to serve no purpose. It is a blackness before which we can only stand mute.

In this respect it is one thing for us to make our own suffering part of our life in service to God; it is quite another to make another's suffering part of his or her service to God. Yet even where one's own suffering is concerned, it is possible to be "too understanding." Indeed, in *Suffering Presence* I argued that Christians are under no obligation to interpret all their misfortunes by identifying them with Christ's cross.[48] I did so not only because such identification can be self-deceptive, but also because, more importantly, it can trivialize Christ's cross by making it a generalized symbol of the inexplicability of suffering.[49] The cross was not inex-

---

48. Hauerwas, *Suffering Presence: Theological Reflections on Medicine, the Church, and the Mentally Handicapped* (Notre Dame: University of Notre Dame Press, 1986), pp. 30-36.

49. Rowan Crews notes, "The connection between Christ's suffering and our own suffering is not an easy one to make. Yet such a connection is what the sacramental liturgies intend; not, however, as an act of description or *transformation.* As do all instances of petition and praise, they invoke the presence and action of God. The sacramental liturgy is doxological, not explicative language. God is petitioned to conform the sufferer—as jagged, absurd, and capricious as his or her

plicable; it was the expected response to the political and moral challenge posed by Jesus' proclamation of the kingdom. So I argued that there is no justification for Christians to accept suffering that is avoidable or can be remedied (such as suffering resulting from illnesses, particularly the illnesses of others) with the attitude that such suffering is "my cross to bear."

Yet I received a letter from a friend who raised a significant objection to my argument. She said she was initially persuaded by the argument because, having been raised Catholic, she had been taught to accept suffering, to offer it up for sins, and to consider it a share in the cross of Christ. Reading my account of Christ's cross helped her see the abuses of that approach; nonetheless, after she herself became ill, she somehow felt cheated by my argument. In the end she re-embraced essentially what she had been taught, as she explained to me in some detail:

1 What does it mean to be a Christian when one is sick or suffering in some other way that makes one unable to participate in Christ's ministry? You have written very helpful things about how to be a Christian community for those who are sick. But how does the sick one participate in the

---

situation may be—to Christ's death and resurrection. The sacramental liturgy leaves to God the manner and process whereby this confirmation—which is nothing other than the fulfillment of baptism—is brought about. Thus it may be that the cancer patient, stricken with a form of suffering obviously different from crucifixion, comes nevertheless to discover in the sacramental *anamnesis* of the cross what her death may become and the way to do her own dying. The connection between her death and Christ's death would be made through worship and indeed as an act of worship" ("The Praise of God and the Problem of Evil," pp. 202-3).

Christian life? I found that when I couldn't do the things I think of as Christian ministry I had to reconsider what it meant to be a Christian.

2 I went back to the idea that being a Christian is essentially to be an imitator of Christ. When you have strength and opportunity to confront the powers, that is one way to imitate Christ, and is a very important one, to be sure. But when you can't preach, or teach, or confront, and you can only suffer, it is still possible to imitate Christ by bearing sufferings patiently and without cursing God or neighbor. Those three hours of patience and forgiveness are just as important a part of Jesus' life as were the confrontations with the authorities that got him there. To follow him in this when it is the only part of his life one is able to follow is surely just as important as faithful following in more active ways.

3 Thus, simply having suffering is not part of being Christian, but bearing it patiently ("absorbing evil"), especially for the sake of others, is an important part of being Christian. So long as this difference is kept in mind, sick people ought to be encouraged to interpret their suffering in terms of Christ's cross. If Jesus' patient suffering is the only part of his life available for them to identify with, that possibility should not be taken away from them due to the differences in the causes for the suffering. After all, we are not individually to be complete imitators of Christ; rather, the whole church is. Let those who are well confront the powers and *earn* their crosses; those who are not will have to get theirs for free.

I am sure my friend is right about this. There is no reason why even the suffering we undergo from illness, suffering that seems to have no good reason to exist, cannot be

[88]

made part of the telos of our service to one another in and outside the Christian community. For example, the very willingness of those who are suffering from illness to be in the presence of the well is a form of service. Suffering and pain make us vulnerable, and often we try to protect ourselves by attempting to be "self-sufficient." The willingness to be present as well as to accept the assistance of others when we need help is a gift we give one another. The trick, of course, is to be the kind of community in which such a gift does not become the occasion for manipulating each other, for trying to obtain through our weakness what we cannot get others to give us voluntarily.

It is crucial for us to recognize, however, that while it is perfectly appropriate for us to discover the suffering we experience in illness to have a telos in our service to one another in faith, it is not appropriate for us to try to force that account on another. When we do that we can force pointless suffering and pain into a teleological pattern that cannot help but be destructive. If we try to attribute these terrible results to God's secret providence, that cannot help but make God at best a tyrant and at worst a cosmic torturer. What we must finally do in the face of the suffering of the Carol Wanderhopes is to show the patience that does not try to discern any "purpose" behind the suffering, but without in any way caring less for them.

I am aware that this cannot help but appear to be a hard counsel for those faced with a child's suffering and death, yet I think there is no other humane alternative. As I suggested at the beginning of this section, all we can do is call on the best wisdom we have developed as a Christ-formed people to help us know how to do this. We must, for example, attend to stories like that of Penny Giesbrecht and her son Jeremy. Her book, which tells the story of

Jeremy's autistic-like behavior, is tellingly titled *Where Is God When a Child Suffers?*[50]

Penny begins her book by evoking a sense of nostalgia—she grew up in Rose City, Minnesota, a community that not only resembles but could indeed *be* Garrison Keillor's Lake Wobegon. Indeed, everything about her early life is almost too perfect. Raised in a conservative Christian home, she decided to attend the non-accredited Oak Hills Bible College because of its heavy emphasis on the study of the Bible. There she fell in love with Tim Giesbrecht, who came from an equally conservative Christian home. She and Tim married after graduation.

Once, while she and Tim were visiting Tim's family, the subject of evil came up in a rather odd manner:

> Tim's father, a kindly man in his early sixties, loved to talk about God. One evening we were having tea after dinner and I mentioned that whenever there was a thunderstorm my parents asked us to sleep downstairs on the floor—just in case of fire. Tim's father was obviously shocked. "Don't they have faith in God?" he asked.
>
> "Well, yeah," I mumbled, "but that doesn't mean nothing bad will ever happen to you, or that you shouldn't take precautions." Tim's father quoted Bible verses about trusting God and being held in the palm of his hand. I thought of my cousin's death, but [I] . . . said nothing.
>
> At Oak Hills we often discussed the problem of evil. "Mr. T.," as we called Mr. Thompson, the president of Oak Hills, was a deeply intelligent and logical man. Under his leadership the faculty pushed us to understand who God was for

---

50. Giesbrecht, *Where Is God When a Child Suffers?* (Hannibal, Mo.: Hannibal Books, 1988). All subsequent references to her book will appear parenthetically in the text.

ourselves, instead of blindly accepting the traditions of our heritage. We came to believe that the free will of humankind was really free. For the first time I understood I could make true choices, that God could work through my choices, that in fact He had chosen to do just that. I also began to understand that evil resulted from sinful humanity, that our capacity to choose between good things was also a capacity to make bad choices which often resulted in sufferings for ourselves and others. When I graduated from Oak Hills I had made huge strides in intellectualizing about the problem of evil. I continued to pray and think, however, as if God were the Big Santa Claus in the sky. Old habits and ways of thinking are very difficult to break. (pp. 16-17)

But early in her life Penny—and Tim—had no reason to think differently. For the first two years of their marriage, Tim worked as a manager of a security firm in Canada. Then, feeling a desire to be more closely involved in Christian ministry, he entered Northwestern College in St. Paul to study to become a Christian radio broadcaster. Penny decided to begin a Christian day-care center, and that business helped to support the two of them while Tim was a student. Not long after this transition, Penny had their first child, Jeremy, which means "chosen by Jehovah."

But Penny's ideas of God and evil did not remain unchallenged. During one of Jeremy's early childhood illnesses (a combination of pneumonia and an ear infection), Penny, frightened that Jeremy might die, found herself praying for answers:

"How does it all fit? Are You trying to warn me not to love Jeremy too much? Jesus, what can I do? I want to trust Jeremy's life with You, yet I don't understand what it is I should believe." My head folded over Jeremy's sleeping white form as I sat in the now empty and dimly lit waiting room. "Dear God in Heaven, what did I do to lose Your blessing? Every day I pray for Your protection for my son. Why is this happening to us?" My war with God continued until all of my arguments had been stated. Finally, spent, I sat resigned. "I've no one else to turn to. I don't understand anything about how You work. But, even if You do call children home . . . even if You call Jeremy home, You're all I've got. I choose to trust You." A measure of peace overcame me. I was tired of fighting. (p. 24)

After learning that Jeremy had spinal meningitis, however, Penny says she suddenly felt rudely shoved from the naiveté of childhood into the reality of adulthood. "I'm only twenty-two years old! I'm too young to have to deal with this" (p. 25). Yet Jeremy recovered, which gave Penny the feeling that "nothing is going to happen to our baby after all. God is good. He's watching over Jeremy. Nothing bad is going to happen! Nothing!" (p. 29).

But something was wrong with Jeremy. After developing well through his first two years, he began to regress, no longer using words he once did. He related to his new sister, Charity Joy, but he was increasingly withdrawn around other children. Thus began the search for "what was wrong" as well as a proper context for Jeremy's schooling. Finally Jeremy was diagnosed as "autistic-like," a condition which proved even worse than autism, since he did not even respond to the forms of positive reinforcement used to keep autistic children from further regression. The Giesbrechts' church meant a great deal to them, but Jeremy was hard to handle even there: one year he upset the Christmas program by running around the church in an uncontrolled fashion.

Things did not get better—only worse. The Giesbrechts did their best to cope. Tim, feeling the need to be of more immediate support, began to help Penny run the day-care center. They were wonderfully supported by their minister and their church. And they began to face the fact that Jeremy would never get better. As Tim wrote to his parents, "Just because we are Christians does not mean we are immune to illness. We have to face the fact that Jeremy may never get better. Even though Jeremy isn't normal he is a sweet boy and we love him very much just the way he is" (p. 74). Yet Penny confesses that both she and Tim were exhausted— emotionally, physically, and spiritually: "We had followed every medical lead. We had done all we knew. Our spirits were weary after two grueling years of unanswered questions. But finally we decided to give God the opportunity to heal Jeremy and glorify Himself if He chose to." The pastor led a healing service for Jeremy, beginning with a prayer:

> "Lord, here we are asking you for healing for this one. We believe you have the power. You have told us to call deacons, to anoint with oil, and ask for healing. In your name we ask you, heal Jeremy if it be your will." Tim then spoke and explained Jeremy's illness holding his face in his hands and sobbing. I was glad I had sat next to him so I could hold his hand now. We shared our pain. Electric is what they call the air when realness is sensed, when masks are laid down and one becomes broken before God. Why is it we so seldom become vulnerable to one another? Does it happen only out of dreadful pain? I wondered. (p. 75)

But the Giesbrechts' troubles were only to worsen. Just as they were beginning to maintain a normal life given Jeremy's condition, his legs were severely burned when his pants caught fire from the burner on their electric stove. In the ambulance on the way to the hospital, Penny, torn by Jeremy's anguished cries, was inconsolable:

I could not be comforted. "We're good parents, God! Things
like this don't happen to parents who watch their children!
We prayed even today you'd protect Jeremy! Jeremy can't
talk! Isn't that enough, God?" The last shred of my childhood belief that God would protect me and mine if we fully
trusted Him fragmented before my eyes. Aloneness and
despair filled me up. I did not feel God's presence yet I
continued to call on his name. "God! Jesus! Help our baby!"
I searched for a way to escape the reality at my knees. My
mother's heart cried, "Let me die! Let me and Jeremy die
in this ambulance! Let us out! Jeremy has beautiful legs!
We haven't even had our lunch yet! Let us go back and do
it over again. We'll eat lunch and think about it calmly.
Dear God! Give us another chance! We won't let it happen
if we can just go back and do it over again!" (p. 82)

The rest of the book relates the Giesbrechts' extraordinary struggle to save Jeremy with the help of the St. Paul
Ramsey Medical Center and the staff of its burn center. In
a chapter called "The Bond of Suffering," Penny describes
the support they received from the other patients and their
families at the center. Before Jeremy finally began to recover,
he endured over a year of failed skin grafts and infections.
During this time the Giesbrechts learned how deep the
compassion of their community was, receiving not only
monetary aid but also constant personal support.

Because of their exemplary care of Jeremy, Tim and
Penny were asked to return to Oak Hills Bible College to
lead a seminar entitled "When a Child Suffers." They had
worked through many false reasons others had offered to
explain why Jeremy was suffering—so that they could grow
spiritually; so that God could be glorified; so that their
values would be made more Christ-like; so that love and
community would be fostered among believers; so that they

would know how to help others who suffer—all of which make God the ultimate sadist. Now they had some other ideas to offer, as Penny explained at the seminar:

> When Tim and I realized that God wasn't pulling strings to allow suffering in the life of Jeremy, specifically, we were freed to really love God. Suffering is a result of the world we live in. God isn't doing it. We know that many of you here today are hurting. For others of you, life is going along right according to schedule. You may think, "This isn't relevant for me." To you, I offer a challenge: suffering is part of earth-side living. The sufferers are not specially chosen out by God to suffer for a specific reason, any more than you are especially blessed or privileged by Him. When we were students at Oak Hills, Mr. T. challenged us to demand logic from what we believed. We suggest you do the same. Seek truth. It will revolutionize your life. How you pray. How you live. And most particularly, how you comfort the suffering.
>
> Three questions I'd like to leave you with: First, is it possible the belief "that our trust in God will guarantee us health and prosperity" comes only because we are a comfortable, wealthy nation, with access to money and medicine which most of the rest of the world does not have?
>
> Second, are we American Christians more deserving of a comfortable life than our Third World brothers and sisters?
>
> Third, do we want a guarantee of personal protection, good health, and prosperity so badly that we would dare bend our theology to include promises God has never given us? (pp. 159-60)

So ends the Giesbrechts' witness. There is no point to Jeremy's suffering, but his life has a place in Penny and Tim Giesbrecht's lives and finally in God's life. That is, finally, all we can say.

CHAPTER III

Medicine as Theodicy

Death in a Liberal Society

When I speak before lay audiences—that is, before people who are not directly involved with medicine—I ask them how they want to die. I do so because I think no question better illumines how our attitudes shape the form of medical care we receive. The presumption of many—a presumption, I might add, underwritten by many in medicine, since it underwrites their own self-interest—is that medicine is basically a scientifically neutral set of skills at which all well-trained physicians are equally adept. Medicine is seen as a set of means, admittedly a very powerful set of means, that are in themselves value-neutral. The only moral questions that occur concern the use or misuse of those skills. Moral questions about medicine are about what ends those skills should serve.

When we consider how we want to die, we begin to appreciate how this view of medicine and the moral questions surrounding medicine are far too simple. Medicine reflects who we are, what we want, and what we fear. For example, when I ask people how they want to die, they always say, without fail, "painlessly," "quickly," "in my sleep," and "without causing great trouble to those close to me." Such desires seem straightforward and rational. They reflect what any of us would want if we thought about it—namely, we rightly want to die without knowing what is happening to us and without causing great pain to ourselves and others, since we do not want to be a "burden" to others.

Nonetheless, at other times and in other places this understanding of death would have been considered irrational if not immoral. For example, medieval persons most feared a sudden death, a death that would not allow them to make proper spiritual preparation. Elaine Tierney notes that in the thirteenth century "popular preaching instructed parishioners to remember death. Gottfried writes that 'preachers advised people to go to sleep every night as if it was their last and as if their beds were their tombs.' Thomas à Kempis wrote of death: 'He who is dead to the world, is not in the world, but in God, unto whom he lives, comfortable, and your life is hid with Christ in God.' The preparation for death was important. To die without having confessed one's sins would submit one to eternal damnation. So the emphasis was upon death and from this developed the concept of dying well and the guides that described the 'art of dying.'"[1]

The medieval world preferred those illnesses that gave

---

1. Tierney, "Death and Dying in the Renaissance: An Analysis of Northern European Hospital Painting." Unpublished paper presented at the 1987 meeting of the Society for Religion and Medicine in New Orleans.

one a lingering death or at least time to prepare for one's death. It is interesting to speculate whether cancer would have posed the same threat to that world which it does to ours. For our desire to "cure" cancer springs not only from the large number of people who actually get cancer but also from the fact that cancer challenges our very conceptions of how we would like to die. Our understanding of violent death is based on those same conceptions. The medieval person could look forward to dying in war, since there was time prior to battle to prepare for potential death. We prefer to die in unanticipated automobile accidents.

Our medicine, moreover, reflects the way we think about death. There are few things on which we as a society agree, but almost everyone agrees that death is a very unfortunate aspect of the human condition which should be avoided at all costs. We have no communal sense of a good death, and as a result death threatens us, since it represents our absolute loneliness. Michael Ignatieff offers this observation:

> As secular people we may claim that ultimate questions about the ends of human life are unanswerable in principle and therefore no business of ours, but each one of us has our hour of need. However blind life on the spiral may be, there is one hour when it all stops. What then will we say? What then will we need?
>
> . . . We no longer share a vision of the good death. Most other cultures, including many primitive ones whom we have subjugated to our reason and our technology, enfold their members in an art of dying as in an art of living. But we have left these awesome tasks of culture to private choice. Some of us face our deaths with a rosary, some with a curse, some in company, some alone. Some die bravely, to give courage to the living, while others die with no other audience than their lonely selves. Some of

us need a cosmology in which we can see the spark that is our life, and some of us go to our deaths needing nothing more than the gaze of another to console us in the hour of our departing.[2]

Ignatieff offers further comment on this phenomenon:

What would astonish a primitive tribesman about the state of our spirits is that we believe we can establish the meaningfulness of our private existence in the absence of any collective cosmology or teleology. . . . We share with other tribes the idea that certain forms of knowledge are necessary to our health, but we are the only tribe which believes that such necessary knowledge can be private knowledge—the science of the individual. We have created a new need, the need to live an examined life; we pursue its satisfaction in the full babble of conflicting opinions about what life is for, and we pursue it in a collectively held silence about the meaning of death. . . .

Without knowing it, we have been living this way for a very long time, at least since the European Enlightenment. It was then that philosophers began to try, by their own example and by their writing, to demonstrate that a secular market society could provide competitive individuals with sufficient reasons for co-operating, and for living.[3]

What can sustain such cooperation is our willingness to enter into a compact with one another through which we agree not to raise issues about what our lives ought to be about; the compact is based on our mutual desire to avoid death and, in particular, the knowledge that we will have to die. We thus

---

2. Ignatieff, *The Needs of Strangers* (New York: Viking, 1985), pp. 76-77.
3. Ignatieff, *The Needs of Strangers*, p. 79.

conspire to hide our deaths from ourselves and from one another, calling our conspiracy "respect for the individual."

The Limits of Medicine: Callahan's Case

Medicine cannot help but become part of this conspiracy; indeed, now the task of medicine is to go to elaborate lengths to keep us alive, the consequence being that some of us end up being mere physical shells incapable, when we are dying, of *knowing* we are dying. Because cure, not care, has become medicine's primary purpose, physicians have become warriors engaged in combat with the ultimate adversary—death.[4] Of course, since this is a war that cannot be won, it puts physicians in a peculiar double bind. They must do everything they can to keep us alive, as if living were an end in itself, but then they must endure our blame when, inevitably, they fail. Almost as perplexing is the fact that although doctors are obligated to use every possible medical technology to keep us alive in order to insure that we will die "only when everything possible has been done," we complain that doctors go to unreasonable lengths to keep us alive.

Our attitude toward death and our corresponding conception of medicine has created a problem: Given our boundless expectations of medicine, how can we ever set limits on medical care? In our society of strangers, who are held together only by the presumption that any individual need is

---

4. For an illuminating analysis of the limits as well as the possibilities of this image of the physician, see William May's *The Physician's Covenant: Images of the Healer in Medical Ethics* (Philadelphia: Westminster Press, 1983), pp. 63-86.

legitimate as long as it does not unduly impede others from pursuing the satisfaction of *their* needs, there seems to be no limit to the needs that medicine can be asked to serve. In such a context, medicine is in danger of being used as a means to eliminate all those "evils" which we believe are arbitrary because we presume that it is our task as humans to make our existence safe from outrageous fortune.[5] What we cannot do, it seems, is set limits on this project, since any such limits themselves seem arbitrary and thus unfair.

In *Setting Limits: Medical Goals in an Aging Society,* Daniel Callahan illumines this dilemma (as well as manifests the difficulties it creates) through his proposals about how we might manage it.[6] The dilemma has, of course, been caused by medicine's redefinition of aging and death. Once concepts such as "old," "aging," and "premature death" gained their meaning from the social and moral responsibilities inherent in the practices of a community; now these concepts are defined by "the state-of-the-art of medicine at any given moment" (p. 56). This transition makes it hard to determine what expectations the elderly should have for their own health and life as well as how those expectations should be understood in relation to other societal needs. Currently the expectations of the elderly are high and becoming higher.

---

5. For a stimulating analysis of the role of "luck" in Greek moral reflection, see Martha Nussbaum's *The Fragility of Goodness* (Cambridge: Cambridge University Press, 1986).

6. Callahan, *Setting Limits: Medical Goals in an Aging Society* (New York: Simon & Schuster, 1987). All subsequent references to Callahan's book will appear parenthetically in the text. For critiques of Callahan, see David Thomasma, "Moving the Aged into the House of the Dead: A Critique of Ageist Social Policy," *Journal of American Geriatrics Society* 37 (Feb. 1989): 169-72; and Joseph Fletcher, "Ethics and Old Age," *Update* 4 (June 1988): 2-5.

From a social point of view that considers equitable distribution of health-care benefits, the statistics are sobering, as Callahan notes: "In 1980, the 11 percent of our population over age 65 consumed some 29 percent of the total American health-care expenditures of $219.4 billion. By 1984, the percentage had increased to 31 percent and total expenditures to $387 billion" (p. 119). This trend, moreover, shows no signs of changing. According to current projections, by 2040 the elderly will constitute 21 percent of our general population and consume 45 percent of all public support for health care. The problem, in short, is that a large percentage of the total health-care dollar in our society is spent caring for the elderly—and an equally large percentage of that is consumed during the last year of life.

Given this situation, Callahan argues that we have no alternative but to consider some kind of rationing of the resources we use to care for the elderly. This must come at the level of national policy rather than at the bedside because of the uncertainty of prognosis: "Can physicians ordinarily (save at the last moment) *know* that an elderly person is dying and that further sophisticated medical care will do the patient no significant good? Apparently not." One procedure leads to another, with the result that more and more money is spent, often with little or no good result. Yet given the commitment of the individual physician to care for the individual patient, it is impossible to ask him or her to do otherwise (p. 131).

As a counteraction, priorities must be set, as Callahan explains:

Where there is now a powerful bias in favor of innovative medical technology, and a correspondingly insatiable appetite for more of it, that will have to be replaced by a bias in the other direction where the aged are concerned. The alternative bias should be this: that no new technologies should be developed or applied to the old that are likely to produce only chronic illness and a short life, to increase the present burden of chronic illness, or to extend the lives of the elderly but offer no significant improvement in their quality of life. Put somewhat differently, no technology should be developed or applied to the elderly that does not promise great and inexpensive improvement in the quality of their lives, no matter how promising for life extension. Forthright government declarations that Medicare reimbursement will not be available for technologies that do not achieve a high, very high, standard of efficacy would discourage development of marginally beneficial items. (p. 143)

Callahan notes that such a policy cannot help but appear prejudicial against the aged unless as a society we are able to regain a sense of a "natural life span." This means that we must recapture a "biographical vantage point" toward our lives that allows us to fit our lives within an ongoing narrative in such a way that death seems natural and expected at a certain juncture. Callahan explains it this way: "No precise chronological age can readily be set for determining when a natural life span has been achieved—biographies vary—but it would normally be expected by the late 70s or early 80s. While a person's history may not be complete—time is always open-ended—most of it will have been achieved by that stage of life. It will be a full biography, even if more details are still to be added. Death beyond that period is not now, nor should it be, typically considered premature or untimely" (p. 172). Viewing life this way should also mean that the care we expect at one point in our lives should not be the care we expect at another:

"The existence of medical technologies capable of extending the lives of the elderly who have lived out a natural life span creates no presumption whatever that the technologies must be used for that purpose. . . . Medicine should in particular resist the tendency to provide to the aged the life-extending capabilities of technologies developed primarily to help younger people avoid premature and untimely death" (p. 173).

While he is careful to leave decisions open to the individual, Callahan urges us as a society to recover a sense of "tolerable death" so that our deaths might no longer be determined solely by the fact that "the doctor cannot do anything further to extend our lives." Callahan defines a "tolerable death" this way: "the individual event of death at that stage in a life span when (a) one's life possibilities have on the whole been accomplished; (b) one's moral obligations to those for whom one has had responsibility have been discharged; and (c) one's death will not seem to others an offense to sense or sensibility, or tempt others to despair and rage at the finitude of human existence" (p. 66). Attempts to determine appropriate treatment in individual cases should be determined by this framework.

Callahan rightly notes that one of the obstacles to our developing a sense of a "natural life span" and a "tolerable death" is the inherent individualism of our society. Any account of our lives from the "biographical vantage point" requires an understanding of intergenerational responsibilities, what the young owe the aged and vice versa, that our individualism tends to undermine. We are far more comfortable worrying about improving the lot of individuals than coping with intergenerational responsibilities: "The place of the elderly in a good society is a communal, not only an individual, question. It goes unexplored in a culture that does not easily speak the language of community and mutual responsibility. The demands of our interest-group political life constitute another obstacle. It places a high premium on a single-minded pursuit of the interests of particular groups or causes. That is where the usual political rewards are to be found. It is most at home using the language of individual rights as part of its campaigns, and can rarely afford the luxury of publicly recognizing the competing needs of other groups" (p. 220). Callahan goes on to target what is perhaps the biggest stumbling block: "Yet the greatest obstacle may be our almost utter inability to find a meaningful place in public discourse for suffering and decline in life. They are recognized only as enemies to be fought: with science, with social programs, and with a supreme optimism that with sufficient energy and imagination they can be overcome. We have created a way of life that can only leave serious questions of limits, finitude, the proper ends of human life, of evil and suffering, in the realm of the private self or of religion; they are thus treated as incorrigibly subjective or merely pietistic" (p. 220).

According to Callahan, if we are to overcome these obstacles, we must "try to enter into a pervasive cultural agreement to alter our perception of death as an enemy to be held off at all costs to its being, instead, a condition of life to be accepted, if not for our own sake then for that of others" (p. 223). This will, of course, force a corresponding change in our understanding of medicine. For, as Callahan points out, "Medicine is perhaps the last and purest bastion of Enlightenment dreams, tying together reason, science, and the dream of unlimited human possibilities. There is nothing, it is held, that in principle cannot be done and, given suitable caution, little that ought not to be done. Nature, including the body, is seen as infinitely manipulable and plastic to human contrivance. When that conception of

medicine is set in the social context of an individualism
which is, in principle, opposed to a public consensus about
any ultimate human good, it is a potent engine of endless,
never-satisfied progress" (pp. 60-61).

What we must try to recover, says Callahan, is a sense
of medicine as a means to help people "live out a full and
natural life span, not simply more life without discernible
end" (p. 223). Yet Callahan seems to want medicine to do
this without sacrificing any of the gains that have resulted
from the development of modern medicine. He begins this
book by noting that "for most of its history medicine was
relatively powerless to do much about illness, disease, and
death." Only in the twentieth century has medicine been
able to "offer real cures," which has underwritten the general
public's ambition to provide such cures. Thus curing, not
caring, has become the primary end of medicine (p. 15). The
message which medicine now wants us to accept is that "it
is no longer luck or chance that some live and some die but,
instead, simply a failure of science yet to succeed in managing or conquering those illnesses which remain" (p. 16). As
a result, we have come to believe that what *can* be done
medically *ought* to be done. Medicine has become our means
of overcoming our "fragility."

I do not doubt the accuracy of Callahan's account of
the change in our perspective on illness and health which
modern medicine at once reflects and underwrites. Moreover,
like him, I am sure that most of us remain profoundly
ambivalent about that change, because as we sense that we
are reaching limits, of which the resources expended on the
elderly are but the most graphic example, we do not want
to sacrifice the genuine gains that have been made. Yet it is
unclear how we can change our understanding of the ends
we want medicine to serve without experiencing some loss.

In a way, modern medicine exemplifies the predicament of the Enlightenment project, which hopes to make society a collection of individuals free from the bonds of necessity other than those we choose. In many ways that project has been accomplished, only now we have discovered that the very freedom we sought has, ironically, become a kind of bondage. Put in the language of theodicy, we now suffer from the means we tried to use to eliminate suffering.

I am also convinced that Callahan is right to think that we need to recover a more limited and modest conception of medicine. In order to do that, however, we need a better understanding of the illnesses which we think justify medical intervention. Without that, we cannot help but allow medicine, whose rationale and form must always be in terms of service, to become an end in itself rather than a kind of service. If medicine is to serve our needs rather than determine our needs, then we must recover a sense of how even our illnesses fit within an ongoing narrative. The crucial question concerns what such a narrative is to be, so that we can learn to live with our illnesses without giving them false meaning.

That we need to construe life as a narrative is what I think Callahan is suggesting when he discusses our need to recover a sense of a "natural life span" and a sense of a "tolerable death." His definitions of these terms seem not only reasonable but humane. The problem with Callahan's recommendation for a recovery of these notions is that such concepts remain far too formal. He talks, for example, about having "one's life possibilities accomplished," but what precisely does that mean? I should like to live long enough to have read all of Trollope's novels twice—but even if I accomplished that, I suspect I would want a try at three times. Similarly, he talks about one's having discharged his/her moral obligations to others—but when are these obligations ever fully discharged? The elderly never cease to carry with them the cumulative wisdom of their culture and their lives, which is a significant gift they can give to the young. Callahan also defines a tolerable death as one that does not offend the "sense or sensibility" of others. But in the end the crucial issue is not whether one's death seems offensive to others, but rather the kind of expectations we ought to have so that death, perhaps even an untimely death, is an event to be accepted—accepted with sorrow, but accepted nevertheless.

One has the sense that Callahan is putting forth definitions of a "natural life span" and "tolerable death" in the hope of beginning a conversation necessary to fill in the content of these notions.[7] But, as his own analysis suggests,

---

7. In his recent book entitled *What Kind of Life: The Limits of Medical Progress* (New York: Simon & Schuster, 1990), Callahan's "communitarian" agenda is explicit. Indeed, in a letter he wrote to me he said, "I see both my last two books as trying to work out a kind of communitarian agenda for medicine, and though I have not used the formal language of the debate between liberalism and communitarianism, I decided some time ago that it would be much more interesting to actually try to develop a communitarian perspective with some very real issues rather than write one more theoretical book on the subject. It seems to me that my approach to a 'natural life span' is meant to be thoroughly communitarian, in that I am not interested as such in the fact that you personally have a great agenda of books you would like to read, and that there is no end of possibilities there. I want to say that we need to pool our collective understanding of a reasonable and natural lifespan and then use that to set a general policy applying to all—regardless of individual variations. I think for policy purposes we could not adapt to individual variation, and thus I want communal response. In that sense, it is rather formal, but I think one has to begin working there to develop a consensus, and I would try to base a consensus on

there is little reason to believe this would be possible in a society like ours. For our individualism tends to undermine

some rather common human experience, i.e., the fact that going to funerals of people over the age of 80 is very different from going to the funerals of younger people" (letter dated 12 Feb. 1990).

I admire Callahan's effort in this respect, but I continue to doubt whether we can "collectively" come to agreement about what a "natural life span" should be. For I suspect that that very way of putting the matter betrays liberal political presuppositions which I fear have created the problem in the first place—i.e., that there is something called the individual whose subjective presumptions about the meaning of life now have to be subject to a collective will—the latter now understood as a consensus of individual wills. Put differently, the assumption that we must choose between "liberalism and communitarianism" is a choice determined by liberal presuppositions.

I cannot help but be impressed, however, by Callahan's attempt to develop the moral conversation necessary for American society to come to some reasonable judgments about these matters. To be particularly noted is his observation that the movement for legalizing euthanasia

rests upon precisely the same assumptions about human need, health, and the role of medicine that have created our present crisis—the right to, and necessity of, full control over our fate. Legally available active euthanasia would worsen, not help, that crisis. By assuming that, in the face of a failure of medicine to cure our illness or stop our dying, we should have the right to be killed, the euthanasia movement gives to the value of control over self and nature too high a place at too high a social cost. The contemporary medical enterprise has increasingly become one that considers the triumph of illness and the persistence of death both a human failure and a supreme challenge still to be overcome. It is an enterprise that feeds on hope, that constantly tells itself how much farther it has to go, that takes all progress to date as simply a prologue to the further progress that can be achieved. Nothing less than total control of human nature, the banishment of its illnesses and diseases, seems to be the implicit ultimate goal.

The argument for euthanasia seems to be agreeing about the

the kind of commitments so necessary for a society to comprehend death within an ongoing narrative.

My use of the language of narrative is not simply another conceptual alternative to Callahan's "natural life span" and "tolerable death" but rather an attempt to elicit a different set of social and political presumptions. In particular, it is an attempt to remind us that there is no "solution" to the problem of "setting limits" to medicine as long as the primary presumptions of liberalism are accepted— presumptions that Callahan, I think, continues to accept. For appeals to a "natural life span" and a "tolerable death" underwrite the liberal political presumptions that our lives are ours to do with what we will within our "natural" limits. In contrast, the recognition that our lives are narratively determined is a reminder that insofar as we live well, we more nearly discover rather than create our lives.

Of course, in a sense, little hangs on which concept— "narrative," "natural life span," or "tolerable death"—best helps us comprehend our deaths as part of our lives. What

---

centrality and validity of control as a goal: if medicine cannot now give us the health and continued life we want, it can and should at least give us a total control over the timing and circumstances of our death, bringing its skills to bear to achieve that end. . . .

There is a clear consequence of this view: our slavery to our power over nature is now complete. Euthanasia is, in that respect, the other side of the coin of unlimited medical progress. The compassion it seeks is not just in response to pain and suffering. It is more deeply a response to our failure to achieve final control over our destiny. That is why we cannot be rid of pain. (*What Kind of Life*, pp. 242-43)

It is my contention that the presumptions Callahan rightly attacks in this passage are built into our political ethos and in fact represent our "collective understanding."

is crucial is that the content of the concept be such that the social practices necessary for us to be able to make our deaths part of our life projects are sustained. The appeal to narrative at least has the advantage of reminding us that our lives and our deaths are not occasional bits of unconnected behavior but part of a larger pattern; recognizing this gives purpose to our lives. When such a pattern is thought to be missing, death and illness cannot help but seem pointless and meaningless. As a result, illness and death can be seen only as something to deny.

Stories of Sickness and Death

In his recent book entitled *Stories of Sickness,* Howard Brody has begun to explore the relationship between sickness and narrative.[8] Brody notes that "suffering is produced and

---

8. Brody, *Stories of Sickness* (New Haven: Yale University Press, 1987). For a similar perspective, see Arthur Kleinman, *The Illness Narratives: Suffering, Healing, and the Human Condition* (New York: Basic Books, 1988). Kleinman notes, "One of the core tasks in the effective clinical care of the chronically ill—one whose value it is all too easy to underrate—is to affirm the patient's experience of illness as constituted by lay explanatory models and to negotiate, using the specific terms of those models, an acceptable therapeutic approach. Another core clinical task is the empathetic interpretation of a life story that makes over the illness into the subject matter of a biography. Here the clinician listens to the sick individual's personal myth, a story that gives shape to an illness so as to distance an otherwise fearsome reality" (p. 49).

Kleinman's perspective is in many ways extremely sensitive, and no doubt he is right about the therapeutic process. However, his argument is not philosophically rigorous. He seems to think that the physician's understanding of "disease" can be distinguished from the patient's

alleviated by the meaning one attaches to one's experience. The primary human mechanism for attaching meaning to particular experiences is to tell stories about them. Stories serve to relate individual experiences to the explanatory constructs of the society and culture and also to place the experiences within the context of a particular individual's his-

---

understanding of his or her "illness"; the latter, he claims, is narrative-dependent in a way that the former is not. Yet that clearly cannot be the case. For an argument that the typological characterization of diseases is equally narrative-dependent, see Per Sundstrom, *Icons of Disease: A Philosophical Inquiry into the Semantics, Phenomenology and Ontology of the Clinical Conceptions of Disease* (Kinkoping University: Department of Health and Society, 1987). Sundstrom offers this observation:

In clinical medicine at least our mode of oral production of works of discourse is very much alive, namely, the narration of patient-disease histories. All material differences between patients' narratives notwithstanding, there are common formal genre rules that are more or less diligently adhered to. There is always a story, a succession of events which gain their real significance only as inserted in the whole of the story; the story typically proceeds up till now, till the present encounter with the physician, which marks a new phase in the story; this up-till-now character is there irrespective of whether the story is an exciting one, or just gloomy, or seemingly trivial, etc. These oral "historical" works play a considerable role in generation of the integral clinical conceptions of disease, and not only in their generation but in their very constitution. Narratives are inscribed in textbooks, though not in the unaltered genre form of oral history narratives. The didactic forms, the integration of relevant information from the laboratory sciences, the interest in somehow managing the patient professionally, etc., all these features emanating from the exigencies of the clinical encounter make for a transformation of the genre rules of patient narratives. Some features of patients' narratives are highlighted while others may be more or less ignored because considerations other than "history" are deemed of greater significance for the management of the patient. (p. 178)

tory."9 To label an experience—for example, an act of coward-ice—is to place the experience within a set of practices as well as to see how the experience fits in with the character of the upbringing and the ongoing life of the one having the experience.

Brody argues that medicine is constantly engaged in this process in that it provides the patient with descriptions that turn the experience of illness in a positive direction—thus the ubiquitous "placebo effect" in medicine. Brody distinguishes three closely related components of the placebo effect: "The illness experience must be given an explanation of the sort that will be viewed as acceptable, given the patient's existing belief system and worldview. Second, the patient must perceive that he or she is surrounded by and may rely upon a group of caring individuals. Third, the patient must achieve a sense of mastery or control over the illness experience, either by feeling personally powerful enough to affect the course of events for the better or by feeling that his or her individual powerlessness can be compensated for by the power of some member or members of the caring group (such as the physician)."10

Brody notes that a negative interpretation of illness can have negative results—for example, an individual's death can be predicted in such a fashion that it leads to the withdrawal of family and close friends and the subsequent death of the patient. "In contrast," Brody points out, "the reassuring story that is commonly told by the physician to account for the illness experience ('It looks like you've picked up that virus that is running around town—you're the sixth person I've seen today with exactly the same symptoms'), coupled with

---

9. Brody, *Stories of Sickness,* p. 5.
10. Brody, *Stories of Sickness,* p. 10.

the caring and solicitous attitude of physicians and the reassuring rituals that promise control of events ('Take two aspirins four times a day, gargle with warm salt water every hour, and stay in bed till the fever goes away'), may well effect a speedier recovery than could be accounted for either by the usual spontaneous remission rate of the illness or by the purely pharmacological efficacy of the remedies administered."[11]

Brody is reminding us of something that Paul Ramsey emphasized years ago in his book entitled *The Patient as Person:* that the subject of the physician's art is the patient.[12] The physician's task is not to cure a disease in the abstract, since there are no diseases in the abstract, but to cure Mr. Jones's gall-bladder ailment and Mrs. Smith's cancer of the jaw. As Ramsey put it, "Men's capacity to become joint adventurers in a common cause makes possible a consent to enter the relation of patient to physician or of subject to investigator. This means that *partnership* is a better term than *contract* in conceptualizing the relation between patient and physician or between subject and investigator."[13] Accordingly, Ramsey insisted that medicine is morally formed by the physician's commitment to the overriding good of each patient in a manner in which that good can never be qualified by goods for society and/or future generations exactly because such "a" good is the good of us all.

Of course, Ramsey was well aware that to say this is but to begin the process of discussion and reflection, particularly in matters dealing with death and dying. He raised this issue as an example:

---

11. Brody, *Stories of Sickness,* p. 7.
12. Ramsey, *The Patient as Person: Explorations in Medical Ethics* (New Haven: Yale University Press, 1970).
13. Ramsey, *The Patient as Person,* p. 6.

If in the case of terminal patients the quality of life they can expect enters into the determination of whether even ordinary or customary measures would be beneficial and should or should not be used, cannot the same be said of infants? It is not obvious that an anencephaletic baby should be respirated while a grown man in prolonged coma should no longer be helped to breathe. In the first of life, a human being may be seized by his own unique dying. Indeed, far from taking the death of the aged and the enormous death rate of zygotes and miscarriages to be a part of the problem of evil, a religious man is likely to take this as a sign that the Lord of life has beset us behind and before in this dying life we are called to live and celebrate. There is an acceptable death of the life of all flesh no less in the first than in the last of it. An ethical man may always gird himself to oppose this enemy, but not the religious ethical man.[14]

Ramsey explained further how we are likely to respond when confronted with the death of a loved one, emphasizing the physician's role in the decisions to be made:

Such is the human condition, that all are responsible for all—and in the face of the death of a loved one, we are guilty of many a sin of omission. Out of their guilt, members of the family are likely—at long last—to require that everything possible be done for the hopelessly ill and the dying loved one. At the same time, guilt-ridden people in their grief may be unable to bear the additional burden of a decision to discontinue useless treatment, and they are often relieved if this decision is not wholly placed on them. This means that the physician must exercise the authority he has acquired as a physician and as a man in relation to the relatives and take the lead in suggesting what should be

---

14. Ramsey, *The Patient as Person*, p. 132.

done. In doing this, the doctor acts more as a man than as a medical expert, acknowledging the preeminence of the human relations in which he with these and all other men stand. For this reason, the medical imperative and the moral imperative or permission are, while distinguishable, not separable in the person or in the vocation of the man who is a physician.[15]

There is no doubt that Ramsey's emphasis on the "patient as person" as the central moral presumption of medicine is right. However, we need to know more about what constitutes our "personhood" if we are to understand the nature of medicine as well as how medicine is to be of service to patients. For in Ramsey's account of the matter there is a hint that medicine itself is a battery of technological "fixes" which are to be applied relative to the good of individual patients. Such an account—an account which, I might point out, is a good deal more nuanced in Ramsey's actual analysis of cases—betrays the complexities of the process of clinical medicine and judgment which are noted by Brody.

One of the ways Brody makes his point is by contrasting science with medicine. He notes that science aims "at the discovery of truth, and it succeeds precisely when it discovers a truth, regardless of whether that truth aids any other practical human endeavor outside of science itself." Medicine, on the other hand, "seeks jointly the expansion of knowledge and the use of the knowledge to cure individual patients; but the first aim is in the service of the second, and it is only with actual cure that medicine considers itself to have accomplished its criteria for success."[16]

---

15. Ramsey, *The Patient as Person*, p. 143.
16. Brody, *Stories of Sickness*, p. 32.

If this is right, and I certainly think it is, then the person who is the patient in interaction with the physician should not be seen as a faceless cipher but as an individual with a personal narrative which makes her aware that the very generalized knowledge that the physician commands may, if applied, hurt her. As Brody notes, the "relief of suffering comes most often by changing the meaning of the experience for the sufferer and restoring the disrupted connectedness of the sufferer with herself and with those around her. Indeed, modern medical practice, by focusing so exclusively on bodily pain and ignoring the multiple aspects of personhood and personal meaning, may inadvertently increase suffering while seeking to relieve it."[17] Yet I think our situation is more complex than Brody indicates if, as I suggested previously, our society shares no narrative other than the one that says we must each face death alone.

The Practice of Medicine and the Loss of Narrative

In his article entitled "Narrative Unity and Clinical Judgment," Thomas Long seems to offer an account very similar to Brody's.[18] Yet he comes to quite a different conclusion. Drawing on Alasdair MacIntyre's definition of "practice"—a cooperative activity that has standards of excellence in the pursuit of which "goods internal" to the practice are realized and human powers to achieve excellence are extended—Long suggests that medicine might be con-

---

17. Brody, *Stories of Sickness*, p. 30.
18. Long, "Narrative Unity and Clinical Judgment," in *Theoretical Medicine* 7 (1986): 75-92.

sidered a practice concerned with patients' well-being. Yet he goes on to argue that the goal of medicine cannot be "well-being" in the same way in which the goal of painting can be a good painting. Understanding why this is true will also help us understand why we have so much difficulty establishing appropriate limits for medical care.

Long notes that MacIntyre argues that our lives are not mere chronicity—that is, we are not the kind of beings to whom just one thing after another happens and for whom there is no unity to be discovered that connects those happenings. Accordingly, says MacIntyre, our lives should have a narrative unity. What constitutes this unity? The answer, Long explains, is that the unity of our lives "is the unity of a narrative embodied in a single life. To ask 'What is good for me?' is to ask how best I might live out that unity and bring it to completion! Elsewhere he [MacIntyre] characterizes the unitary life as 'a life that can be conceived and evaluated as a whole.' He speaks of 'the unity of a narrative which links birth to life to death as a narrative beginning to middle to end.'"[19]

Interestingly, a life experienced as a narrative unit is one in which events are not experienced or remembered as foreign. A kind of fatalism in which one's life is seen as fundamentally out of control, in which one is a victim of time, is rendered impotent by a narrative construal, which allows one to integrate one's misfortunes into an ongoing framework. As Long explains, "The terminal disease, the loss of a loved one, a financial loss—all such events, while coming from outside *qua* events, are given significance from within a framework of meaning already in place." Long goes on to explain how this narrative comes into play in medicine:

---

19. Long, "Narrative Unity and Clinical Judgment," p. 79.

To seek a patient's well-being is to presuppose some framework of meaning already in place. Lowering an elderly patient's temperature or controlling his urinary tract infection is not necessarily a contribution to his well-being. The patient may feel better physically, yet be even more unhappy than before his hospital admission. The clinician who seeks the patient's well-being is necessarily constrained by the narrative unity into which he or she has entered. When physicians fail to perceive such unity in their patients' lives (assuming it is present), then clinical medicine, however scientifically well-founded its judgments may be, can enhance patient well-being only by accident. The situation is graver when patients themselves lack any sense of narrative unity, for medicine becomes impotent to bring about or enhance patient well-being, even by accident, if there is no "intelligible narrative" to ground questions about "better or worse" treatments.[20]

According to MacIntyre, it is precisely the notion of life as a narrative unity that modernity undercuts, and in the process it renders the very notion of "sound clinical judgment" problematic. We are unable to answer the question "What would be better (or worse) for this patient?" because any answer to that question "presupposes an ability to identify a real narrative unity constitutive of the patient's life"[21]—and that unity is sometimes absent. This may be because narrative unity grows out of a kind of belief system that not everyone has. Thus MacIntyre notes,

-----

20. Long, "Narrative Unity and Clinical Judgment," p. 80.
21. Long, "Narrative Unity and Clinical Judgment," p. 82. Charles Taylor's account of the "punctual" self in John Locke is a haunting depiction of the way the "self" is viewed in most medical practice. See his *Sources of the Self: The Making of the Modern Identity* (Cambridge: Harvard University Press, 1989), pp. 159-76.

How we treat the aging and the dying and how we ourselves behave as we age and then die will depend in crucial part on what framework of beliefs we possess which enables us to identify aging and dying as particular kinds of social or cosmic events, . . . possessing particular kinds of significance or insignificance. Spinoza's "The free man thinks of nothing less than of dying" cannot be understood except in terms of the whole argument of the *Ethics;* the Catholic Christian who places a skull on his mantlepiece presupposes a quite different set of metaphysical beliefs; and the lady with the blue rinse in Florida who behaves as if she were twenty, but who knows all too well that she is seventy-five, is as frenetic as she is because she does not know what kind of experiences she is undergoing.[22]

Long suggests (following MacIntyre) that in our society we are all a bit like the little old lady with blue hair:

This woman "has" experiences which make no sense to her. She has lost a framework, a feeling for a unity in her life, if she ever had it. Her behavior, dress, and physical appearance all shout self-deception. She is a casualty of "modernity." For a person like this there can be no sound clinical medicine, though scientific medicine may be able to make correct judgments about the proper treatment of any disease she develops. But this latter type of judgment is directed to the disease simply as an instance of a kind, not to the disease as present in *this person.* Only when the process of clinical judgment is personalized, that is, when well-being is the issue, will the process itself be complete. In the case of the woman in Florida this process inevitably will be aborted at the purely technical stage. This means that even if medicine

----

22. MacIntyre, "Patients as Agents," in *Philosophical Medical Ethics: Its Nature and Significance,* ed. H. T. Engelhardt, Jr., and Stuart Spicker (Dordrecht: D. Reidel, 1977), p. 210.

succeeds in curing her disease, this will be simply another event in a life so disordered that she is unable to accept the past as past (she "behaves as if she were twenty").[23]

Of course, it may be objected that it is quite unfair to suggest that this woman is a typical representative of our society. Yet the validity of the suggestion is clear if we juxtapose it with another quote from MacIntyre about our death. He says, "If I have work to do in the world, the time will come when it is done; and when that time comes it is right to die. . . . Each of us is permitted to occupy a certain space in time, a certain role in history; without that particular place and role our lives would be without significance. To recognize that it is our particularity and finitude that gives our lives significance can save us from being consumed by that terrible and destructive desire to remain young that preys on so many Americans."[24]

As Long points out, this passage has important implications not only for patients but also for those who practice medicine. Physicians, just like women with blue hair and elderly men who wear girdles, have their way of denying death. Aggressive medicine in the face of terminal illness can be the result of pressure exerted by the patient's family, but it can also be the result of our society's inability to place death in a morally intelligible narrative. In a society such as ours, however, the dangers of practicing such aggressive medicine go beyond reinforcing our fear of finitude. Now the very presupposition that has produced our medicine— the presupposition that our bodies are but objects to our

---

23. Long, "Narrative Unity and Clinical Judgment," p. 83.

24. MacIntyre, quoted by Long in "Narrative Unity and Clinical Judgment," p. 84.

selves—cannot help but reinforce our society's presumption that our lives are fundamentally constituted by chronicity rather than narrative. That is, to the extent that we think of our lives as a series of discrete events which are open to manipulation by ourselves and others, we invite the assumption that our lives, and our suffering, have no point. Our medical technologies have outrun the spiritual resources of our society, which lacks all sense of how life might properly end. That is, of course, exactly the problem that Callahan has rightly diagnosed. His solution, however, may be an attempt to cure the disease by the very disease itself.[25] For the very notion of a "natural life span" sounds like an attempt to let "scientific rationality" determine when we have lived long enough.

---

25. For a fascinating account of the relation between our society's attitudes toward death and the presuppositions of liberal political theory, see Alfred Killilea, *The Politics of Being Mortal* (Lexington: University Press of Kentucky, 1988). It may be unfair to ask Callahan to deal with issues in political theory in a book about medicine, but it is the burden of my case to show how the fear of death is at the heart of the liberal democratic project. From Hobbes to the present, liberalism has been that theory of society which has presupposed that the only thing people have in common is their fear of death even though they share no common understanding of death. So liberalism is that theory of society which is based on the presumption that each of us must die alone. That fear is the only thing we have in common and thus the only basis for cooperation. Medicine cannot help but become subject to that fear as we try to use medicine to prevent our individual deaths. That project results in medicine becoming an end in itself rather than serving more determinative ways of life. For an extremely thoughtful essay that deals with these matters, see Harmon Smith, "Dying with Style," *Anglican Theological Review* 70 (1989): 327-45. As Smith observes, "If an important aspect of dying well means dying remembered, then there is a diminished chance for dying well when one's dying is insulated and privatized" (p. 343).

Long, however, suggests that, despite our society's emphasis on interpreting our lives in terms of chronicity, we do have something of a sense of how to link the events of our lives into a story that we can see coming to an end. For Long thinks MacIntyre's "representative" little old lady with blue hair is exaggerated. Such people certainly exist, says Long, but they are not typical of our society. In fact, gerontologists have found that the older people become, the less fearful they are of dying. Indeed, some gerontologists see old age as a time when people attempt to develop a view of their life that makes a type of sense which allows them to attain some control over their dying, if not death itself. Such a history is not a *discovered* narrative in MacIntyre's sense, but what Long calls a "fictionalized history"—that is, a narrative which is the result of "selective attention, emphasis, dim remembrance, and possibly even forgetting. The person makes choices about the importance of persons and events, decides on their meanings, though there may be only a minimal awareness of the resulting order as a partially created one. The finished product is the 'fictionalized' history of a life, neither a lie nor 'the truth,' but instead a work of imagination, evaluation, and memory"[26]—we impose a narrative on our lives of chronicity.

Long fears, however, that even when individuals in our society achieve such a narrative unity—that is, when they sense that their lives have been properly completed so their deaths will not be untimely—they cannot avoid coming into conflict with clinical medicine. Patient and physician become strangers to one another when the latter will not accept death even though the former sees it as the completion of his or her story. Long suggests that we should not be surprised by

---

26. Long, "Narrative Unity and Clinical Judgment," p. 87.

this conflict, since the heavy stress in clinical medicine on combatting disease leaves physicians uncomprehending of a narrative approach to life. Physicians have been taught, after all, to delay endings, not to help patients integrate their illnesses and deaths into an ongoing way of life.

Yet Long thinks it is too much to ask that medicine aid us in plotting our lives. For, as MacIntyre has argued, our ability to have our lives achieve a narrative unity is dependent on our ability to comprehend our deaths. In our society this usually occurs, if at all, only very late in life. And if we haven't begun to think of our lives in a narrative fashion, we can hardly demand that physicians give us "plots."

Therefore, according to Long, medicine should stick to what it does best—namely, alleviating or ridding us of those ills which respond to biochemical or mechanical manipulation. The aim of medicine cannot be the well-being of the patient when such well-being presupposes a sense of the narrative unity that neither the patient nor the physician may have. (Ironically, medical treatment, since it must be restricted to the mechanical, may undermine a patient's ability to maintain the narrative sense of life precisely because it drives him to distraction by procedures that only prolong his dying.) The physician cannot supply what is lacking if a patient does not know who she is. The physician may be able to help the patient cope with her pain, but if the patient lacks any substantive narrative, the physician cannot provide a meaning for ineliminable pain. We thus begin to understand why we are condemned to live out only narratives that we believe to be fiction since we know we are their arbitrary authors—because we lack a shared narrative. As a result, we have no way to set limits to the care we would give one another through medicine.

A gloomy enough conclusion. But when we consider the illness and death of children, I believe we see that our situation is even more fraught with difficulty. Brody and Long, who rightly remind us of how illness fits into our ongoing narratives, still think, with Nietzsche, that such narratives are our own creations. They may be right. That would explain why, since young children have not had the opportunity to "create" such a narrative, we abandon them to the institutional means we have of buying them time—that is, medicine—so that they might acquire a narrative. Such is the only alternative as long as we refuse to believe that we are all, adults and children alike, born into a narrative not of our own making—that is, we are creatures of a gracious God who discover that precisely because we are such we do not have to "make up" our lives.

The Private Worlds of Dying Children

I know of no better way to tie together the themes I have tried to develop in this book than to call attention to Myra Bluebond-Langner's extraordinary account of children dying of leukemia.[27] Her patient and powerful description of the lives of terminally ill children and their families as played out in a pediatric oncology clinic is a vivid testimony

---

27. Bluebond-Langner, *The Private Worlds of Dying Children* (Princeton: Princeton University Press, 1978). All subsequent references will appear parenthetically in the text. I am indebted to Professor Jean Bethke Elshtain for calling my attention to Bluebond-Langner's book. For an imaginative theological commentary on the book, see Terry Tilley, "Dying Children and Sacred Spaces" (Winooski, Vt.: Saint Michael's College, 1989).

to our inability to deal with the death of our children except by trying to "cure" them. Ironically, our feverish attempts to make them well create a conspiracy between the children, the parents, and the hospital staff which insures that such children will finally die alone.

Bluebond-Langner is an anthropologist who gained permission to do an ethnological study over a nine-month period in the department of pediatrics of a large midwestern teaching hospital. She obtained her data through day-to-day interaction with the children, their parents, and the doctors, nurses, and other health staff. Sensing that the children were already experiencing enough stress, deprived already of their ability to function as agents in their illness because parents and health staff had taken over that function in the interest of making the children "well," Bluebond-Langner decided she was not going to make their position worse through her probing. Accordingly, she asked each of the children for permission to speak with them. She explained that she was an anthropologist interested in what children thought and did. She notes that the children usually responded by telling her what they had gone through that day—they would, for example, "exhibit their wounds."[28] She notes, however, that

---

28. Bluebond-Langner explains, "A form of behavior common among terminally ill children, 'exhibition of wounds,' . . . underlines how children try to affect not only the way others see them, but also how they see themselves. By showing where and how they have been poked and prodded, children present themselves to others as sick and find their self-image confirmed. This is further evidenced by the fact that once children internalize this view of self, they no longer use this strategy, except when meeting someone for the first time and wanting, for any number of reasons, to affect the stranger's view of them" (pp. 9-10). To illustrate her point, Bluebond-Langner reports what happened the first time that she visited a boy named Jeffrey. She explained that

"if a child did not want to talk, I did not force the issue. It was the children, not parents or staff, I was interested in. My allegiance was to the children" (p. 246).

She continues, "I believe my relationships with the children were based on mutual trust and understanding, established very early in the relationship, and constantly reinforced through mutual giving, taking, and testing" (p. 246). For example, in contrast to family members and the health-care personnel, she never entered a child's room without asking permission. And when she entered the room, she notes, "I would take my cues from the children. If they wanted to watch TV or color pictures, I watched TV or colored" (p. 246). Often the children would talk to her during these activities; some children asked her to watch TV with them in order to "test the relationship." She explains, "As one eight-year-old boy said to me after I watched for one solid hour without a word, 'All right. You're OK. What do you want to know?'" (p. 247).

Bluebond-Langner's extraordinary ability to establish relationships with these children and her resulting study reflect her profound respect for the lives of these children. She began her study in order to challenge the general assumption that children are incapable of moral agency. Children often are not told they are dying because it is assumed

---

she was an anthropologist who was interested in what children thought and did. "He responded, as did the other children, by exhibiting his wounds. 'One, two, three, four' *(pointing to two fingers and his right hip).* 'Two were for bone marrows and two were for blood tests'" (p. 174). Early in their illness leukemic children would display such wounds during every encounter. For these children, says Bluebond-Langner, "repetition was extremely important. The children found confirmed in people's reaction to their pronouncement the fact that they differed from other children" (p. 174).

that they are incapable of comprehending the gravity of their situation. Accordingly, the failure of children to ask questions about their illness is interpreted as reflecting their inability to comprehend what is happening to them. Blue-bond-Langner argues, however, that to so perceive the child's situation is to fail to comprehend the "child's role in the initiation and maintenance of social order" (p. 5). The children whom Bluebond-Langner got to know trusted her because she saw them as moral agents who were re-sponding to one another's pain as well as to their parents' fear and grief with extraordinary sensitivity. Her book is but a documentation of the courage of children in the face of death.

Bluebond-Langner attributes her capacity to "see" these children's ability to act on their world to her use of a sym-bolic-interactionist or ethnomethodological perspective. But anyone reading her book knows that no "method" could ever account for her extraordinary ability to see these children as interpreters of and responsible actors in their world. Rather, her ability is grounded in her moral capacity to respect these children's struggle to discover they are dying and the silent conspiracy they enter into with their parents and physicians to protect their parents from the knowledge that they know they are dying. Her book is about how children learn they are dying and how they deal with that knowledge.

According to Bluebond-Langner, early on the children begin to interpret what is happening to them and to behave accordingly:

> For example, a five-year-old boy interprets his mother's cry-ing as indicating that he is very sick. "See my mommy's red nose, that's from me. Everybody cries when they see me. I'm pretty sick." He also notes that he is getting more presents

than his sister. "I get more presents than when I had my tonsils out. My sister gets the same." Finally, he has been behaving in ways that are ordinarily cause for reprimand and finds that he is not reprimanded. In fact, he is rewarded. Following his interpretation of others' behavior toward him, he sees himself as very ill, and he forges a line of action in accord with such a view. He acts the sick role and claims his right on the basis that he is truly ill. For example, Beth, snatching a toy from her sister, said, "Gimme that, I'm the sick one, not you." (p. 9)

Children learn of the seriousness of their disease because they are forced to quickly learn about the world of the seriously ill as well as their place in it—that is, they have to learn about hospitals and doctors. Even though the parents of the leukemic children whom Bluebond-Langner got to know tried to keep their children isolated from other patients by keeping them in their rooms, the children rapidly gained information about how the hospital worked. For example, they learned that "the pediatric department was one of several departments in the hospital." They also learned that of the two in-patient floors, one was for new-borns and children under five, and the other was for children who were five and older. "The children differentiated the two groups in terms of 'kids who don't wet the bed' or 'don't wear diapers' as opposed to 'kids who do'" (p. 136). Moreover, the children were aware of the treatment rooms where procedures falling between the minor and the major—such as bone marrows, spinal taps, and lumbar punctures—were carried out. Many of the children even noticed that "if the doctor doesn't want your mother around, he takes you in the treatment room" (p. 137).

Particularly important—and revealing—was the children's sense of social setting, as Bluebond-Langner explains:

A child's failure to discuss his or her prognosis in the presence of adults, compared to open discussion in the presence of other children, is one illustration of the effect of social setting. Since the children interpret death as an inappropriate topic of conversation with adults (evidenced by the adults' reactions when children try to discuss it), and as an appropriate topic with other children (evidenced by their willingness to offer information and answer questions), they refrain from discussing the subject in the presence of adults, but pursue it with peers. This is also true of sex discussions among normal children. Leukemic children often discussed their condition in the place children often go to discuss sex—the bathroom, where adults cannot hear them. Looked at another way, then, we can say that children's pretense in one social setting and their candor in another indicates their ability to make judgments about a situation and to act appropriately. (p. 10)

Terry Tilley corroborates this in his essay entitled "Dying Children and Sacred Space." He points out that although these children had no privacy because of their illness, although they were denied the right to have secrets, in fact they created a secret space where they could meet to share information—namely, the bathroom. "There they could share enough information that they could become aware of the truth despite the pretense they had to keep up in the public spaces. There older children, children who had greater experience with the illness, could act as guides for the younger and/or less experienced children. There in the bathroom pretense was suspended and the children could play the roles of truth-tellers."[29]

Besides becoming acutely aware of how to gain infor-

---

29. Tilley, "Dying Children and Sacred Spaces," p. 14.

mation in the hospital, the children also became acute observers of medical personnel. They quickly established, for example, what they perceived to be the hierarchy of power—hematologists, residents, interns, nurses, and medical students. The children identified the hematologists as "their doctors" because they "make all the decisions. Everybody has to do what they say" (pp. 147-48). Thus, Bluebond-Langner explains, "when a resident or an intern came in to do a procedure and the children had not been told about it in advance, they would often ask if the hematologist told the resident that he could do it" (p. 148). And some of them made further distinctions among the groups in the hierarchy: for example, "some of the children remarked that the interns started I.V.s more often than did residents and medical students," and the more experienced even knew that "the intern was sent [to restart the I.V.] only if the veins were hard to find." Thus the children concluded that an intern was a "real doctor," while a medical student was not (p. 150). Their knowledge of nurses, whether they were R.N.s or L.P.N.s, was equally acute.

Since parents and hospital staff routinely withheld information from the children, it was from other patients that the children learned the most. They could easily distinguish between leukemic and nonleukemic patients: "'They [leukemic patients] come to Monday clinic.'" "'We [leukemic patients] all have the same blood disease. You know Greta, she comes [to the hospital] all the time. Well, she has a blood disease [sickle cell disease] too, but she goes to another clinic'" (p. 155). From other leukemic children they could learn what was happening to them:

CHILD: Is Gene getting vincristine again?
MYRA: Yes, I think so.

CHILD: When I had vincristine the second time I lost my hair. *(Pause.)* Gene gets his hair back real fast. I wish I did. (p. 155)

"Most striking," according to Bluebond-Langner, "in light of what others have said . . . , is that the children did know who was alive and who was dead." She reports these conversations:

TOM: Jennifer died last night. I have the same thing, don't I?
NURSE: But they are giving you different medicines.
TOM: What happens when they run out?
NURSE: Well, maybe they will find more before then.

MARIA: I'm going to play with Luis [a child who died six months earlier] in heaven.

ANDY: I knew Maria died. I saw the cart come for her. They told everyone to go in their rooms. (p. 156)

Bluebond-Langner points out that "even the children who were isolated tended to know a great deal about other children's conditions, often more than the respective parents knew" (p. 156). Generally, however, "the leukemic children knew very little about other leukemics beyond their experiences as fellow sufferers. They knew almost nothing about each other's lives outside the hospital or clinic" (p. 157). Almost everything they learned about one another was mediated through the medium of their common disease.

Being bound together by their common enemy meant that the children learned from each other about the treatment for the disease as well as its progress and prognosis. They knew the specific purposes of different drugs as well as their side effects, particularly if they caused changes in physical appearance. "'Prednisone makes me eat like a pig and act like a brat,'" one child commented. And Bluebond-Langner notes that the children "were conscious of the alopecia that resulted from cytoxan":

CHILD: Don't! *{in response to someone stroking his hair}.* I'm getting cytoxan.

CHILD: *(When other children were discussing what they needed for their Halloween costumes)* I needed a wig for Halloween.
O.T.: What were you?
CHILD: No! I was getting cytoxan. (pp. 158-59)

The children were astute about more serious side effects as well, says Bluebond-Langner. "Many children also remarked that the drugs themselves sometimes created problems requiring as much treatment as the disease: 'There's blood in my pee from the cytoxan and they can't stop it. Maybe the platelets will help.' Some even knew that some drugs were so toxic that one could die from the drugs as easily as from the disease: 'I'm going to die soon. They are trying to help my blood, but it's *{the medicine}* making my liver bad'" (pp. 158-59).

The children also learned to assess their condition according to the medical procedures being performed on them. They knew that a bone-marrow test was required before a new drug was tried—and a new drug usually meant that their condition had worsened. Waiting for the results of this test made the children particularly anxious because they understood the significance of the results, as their conversations indicated:

NURSE: Does it bother you to have a bone marrow?
TED: No. It's waiting for the results.
NURSE: Does it hurt?

TED: No! All you feel is the press. They make it red and use a needle to take it out. Oh, yeah, they numb it first.

MYRA: What's happening?
SCOTT: Not good.
MYRA: What do you mean not good?
SCOTT: *(Putting head in Myra's lap)* I have to have a bone marrow. Dr. Wesley said it's not good. I think Mommy's in there crying. (p. 160)

The children knew that an unexpected bone-marrow test meant that there was a change in their condition and that the change was "not good." They learned "that the disease was a series of relapses and remissions," notes Bluebond-Langner (p. 161), and they learned to read the progress of their disease with extraordinary accuracy.

In addition, Bluebond-Langner points out, "all of the leukemics that I studied knew their prognosis. All knew that they were dying before death was imminent. They did not, however, all express their awareness in the same way. Some children said directly, 'I am going to die,' or 'I'm going to die soon. They are trying to help my blood, but it's (the medication's) making my liver bad.' Other children were less direct. They talked about never going back to school, of not being around for someone's birthday, or of burying dolls that they said looked the way they used to look. All of these forms of expression are indications that the children knew they were dying" (p. 165).

Of course, the children did not realize immediately that they were dying. Indeed, Bluebond-Langner thinks the children actually went through five stages in acquiring the information about the disease, recognizing (1) the illness as serious, (2) the names of the drugs and their side effects, (3) the purposes of treatments and procedures, (4) the dis-

ease as a series of relapses and remissions that do not necessarily lead to death, and (5) the disease as a series of relapses
and remissions that do lead to death (p. 166).[30] As the
children passed through these stages of information, they
also passed through five stages of self-definition: (1) I am
seriously ill, (2) I am seriously ill and will get better, (3) I
am always ill and will get better, (4) I am always ill and
will never get better, and (5) I am dying (p. 169).

According to Bluebond-Langner, there is no mystery
to these stages. For example, as soon as the diagnosis was
made, stage 1 began. The children suddenly received a
"deluge of gifts" and realized that there were certain things
they didn't have to do anymore. "The children were no
longer told that they had to go out and play," Bluebond-
Langner noted, "and in some cases, they were not even sent
to school" (pp. 172-76). Based on these signals, the children
knew something had changed, and grasped the fact that they
were very ill. They entered stage 2, Bluebond-Langner says,
after "they had experienced a remission as well as a few rapid
recoveries from minor disease-related incidents." This made
them believe that, although they were very ill, they would
get better. They entered stage 3 after experiencing their first
relapse; at this juncture they began to think of themselves
as chronically ill. At this stage the children noticed that

---

30. Bluebond-Langner makes it clear that the children progressed
through these stages at varying rates: "A child could remain at a given
stage without passing to the next for what seemed an unusual length of
time. Tom, for example, remained at stage 4 for a year, whereas Jeffrey
remained at stage 4 for only a week. Since passage to stage 5 depended
on the news of another child's death, and none had died after Tom reached
stage 4, he could not pass to stage 5. When Jennifer died, the first child
to die that year, all the children in stage 4, regardless of how long they
had been there, passed to stage 5" (p. 169).

adults were less likely to answer questions about their condition; thus they began to recognize and observe the taboos
on speaking about their disease. To gain information they
learned to rely on "overheard conversations between their
parents and the doctors, between other parents, and between
the doctors"; they began to distrust information that adults
volunteered (p. 180).

The sheer reality of the disease itself intruded more and
more. As the children passed from stage 3 to stage 4, they
recognized that there was never any freedom from pain, that
they were able to do less and less, that fewer and fewer plans
were made because of their illness. Eventually they came to
see themselves as always sick, never to get better. Moreover,
they were increasingly shut off from the "normal world,"
which they tried to maintain contact with. "They did not
want to be in reverse isolation," Bluebond-Langner comments,
"because they feared people would not come to see them. . . .
They anxiously awaited the arrivals of various people: 'When
will Odessa [the R.N.] be here? She's real funny and talks to
me'; 'I think I made Dr. Richards feel bad. He doesn't come
in anymore. I ask too many questions'" (p. 183).

The children were particularly affected when a peer
stopped coming to see them. "As long as there was a valid
reason (e.g., he really did go home) why a peer suddenly
stopped coming by the room or sending a message, the
children remained at stage 4," Bluebond-Langner explains.
"Only on hearing of the death of a peer did the children
realize that the cycle of relapses and remissions did not continue indefinitely. It had a definite end—death" (p. 183).
This precipitated the passage to stage 5.

In stage 5, the children played less with their toys, but
when they did so their play often included references to
disease and death. They placed toys in graves, Bluebond-

Langner observes, and "sedentary activity, especially coloring, increased, but the number of themes decreased. Most pictures dealt with destruction, storms, fires, and other disasters" (p. 185). Yet another thing that changed was "their choice and discussion of literature." Bluebond-Langner reports that the most popular book among the children was *Charlotte's Web,* and the chapter they most wanted read is the one in which Charlotte dies. Even those children who read other books would, "when reading or retelling a story, focus on those aspects of the story that dealt with death, disease, or violence—regardless of whether or not it was the main thrust of the story" (p. 186).

Aware that they were dying, some children "felt they could not speak freely, even with people they trusted, about their awareness of the prognosis. These children would not engage others in a conversation about the prognosis or another child's death. They would simply state their awareness and terminate the discussion. One six-year-old boy announced, 'I'm not going to school anymore,' and turned over on his side, refusing to speak to me. A seven-year-old girl blurted out to her brother, 'I won't be here for your birthday,' and crawled under the sheets" (p. 189). Although such behavior was extreme, almost all the children stopped talking to people close to them. "They would withdraw from family and friends, either through expressions of anger or through silence. 'Then she [Mother] won't cry so much and be sad.' Eventually, even conversations about the disease came to an end. The children asked no questions. They knew the answers. They stopped responding or even listening to others" (p. 196).

That behavior is what Bluebond-Langner sought to understand. She has shown us in an extraordinary way that these children had learned they were dying long before their actual death. Why would they keep such knowledge secret? It is her contention that they did so because they recognized the necessity of their entering into a mutual pretense with their parents as well as the medical staff. By mutual pretense she means that each party understood that the patient was dying, but each agreed to act as if the patient was going to live.[31]

How did this pretense develop? Bluebond-Langner explains the process. "The conditions for development of mutual pretense were present from the moment the children entered the hospital. . . . The staff was already predisposed to keep information from patients. . . . For example, when the children were admitted, the nurses marked the children's charts 'Possible WBC (White Blood Cell) Disease,' the notation for leukemia. This notation was used lest patients or unsuspecting family members inadvertently see the charts and from them learn the diagnoses" (p. 200). The parents soon became willing co-conspirators in this pretense. "When children started to ask probing questions about their condition, the parents began to signal their unwillingness to talk about it. They volunteered very little information and explained as little as possible" (p. 201). Often props were used to help the children sustain a "crucial illusion." For instance, notes Bluebond-Langner, "the children often brought school books to the hospital and would on occasion take them out, as if to say, 'I am going back to school, I am not dying'" (p. 203).

---

31. For her account of mutual pretense, Bluebond-Langner is drawing on the study by Barney Glaser and Anselm Strauss entitled *Awareness of Dying: A Study of Social Interaction* (Chicago: Aldine, 1965). Bluebond-Langner's account is troubling not only because of what it reveals about the effect of such pretense on the children dying of leukemia, but also because it reminds us how much our everyday lives are constituted by such pretense.

As Bluebond-Langner describes it, mutual pretense is a delicate balancing act that always threatens to break down. Thus "when a seven-year-old boy's Christmas presents arrived three weeks early and Santa came to visit him," the suggestion was clearly that he would not live to see Christmas. Yet the boy saved the situation by telling "his choked-up family" and the staff members present, "'Santa has lots of children to see, he just came here first'" (p. 204). Bluebond-Langner also observes that even the safest topic could backfire. For example, "a nurse was talking to one seven-year-old boy about baseball players, and he said, 'I can't play baseball any more.' She was able to maintain the mutual pretense context by quickly rejoining, 'That's right, no ball playing in the rooms—hospital rules.' The child could then not follow, as she feared he might, with 'because I'm dying,' and thereby break the mutual pretense" (p. 204).

Bluebond-Langner argues that the oft-made explanation for mutual pretense—namely, that death is a taboo subject—is inadequate to explain the complexity of mutual pretense. Rather, everyone involved in the situation she documents—child, parent, doctor, nurse—was drawn into mutual pretense "because it offered each of them a way to fulfill the roles and responsibilities necessary for maintaining membership in the society, in the face of that which threatened the fulfillment of social obligations and continued membership" (p. 210).

In American society the primary task of children is to grow up. We raise them so that they will "turn out right." One of the primary shaping factors in their lives is going to school: it is one of the principal marks of childhood, just as having a job is one of the principal marks of adulthood (p. 212). Yet, as Bluebond-Langner observes, dying children cannot fulfill their fundamental task to have a future. "They

do not go to school," she points out, "they go to a hospital."
They are not disciplined because there is no point to it. They
are, in effect, like the elderly—"without futures, worried,
often passive, unhappy, and burdened with responsibilities
for others and their feelings." It is no wonder they feel
burdened. "By practicing the rules of mutual pretense," says
Bluebond-Langner, "these children keep the parent/child,
doctor/patient relationship from breaking down. By assuming the role of child or patient, as adults define it, they allow
the parent or doctor to assume the reciprocal role and all
the behavior that follows from it. . . . By practicing mutual
pretense, they demonstrate awareness of their social obligations and responsibilities and their competence in social
relations" (pp. 213-14).

Parents have an equally powerful motivation to enter
into mutual pretense, because the terminal illness takes
away and makes impossible their roles as guardians and
protectors of their children. Like the doctors, parents stand
helpless before the disease. But mutual pretense can help
restore their roles. For example, some parents feel that they
must protect their children from knowledge of the prognosis, and mutual pretense lets them do this by sanctioning
the withholding of information and the offering of decep-
tive comments about "getting better." Of course, as Bluebond-Langner points out, parents are even more threatened
by the prospect of final separation from their children, and
mutual pretense also helps prepare them for this eventu-
ality: "To some extent, mutual pretense helped parents
prepare for this final severance by pacing it out, and by
allowing them to rehearse the separation in an acceptable
manner. By their use of distancing strategies [such as yell-
ing at a parent], children gave parents an excuse [for
terminating a visit]; parents could then leave without feel-

ing they were deserting the children, who, by their actions, were asking them to leave. . . . Also, if a procedure then occurred while the parents were out of the room, as was often the case, they did not have to feel that they had failed to protect the children" (pp. 216-17). One of the most poignant conversations that Bluebond-Langner reports is a short exchange between herself, a child named Jeffrey, and his mother:

MYRA: Jeffrey, why do you always yell at your mother?
JEFFREY: Then she won't miss me when I'm gone.
MRS. ANDREWS: Jeffrey yells at me because he knows I can't take it. He yells so I can have an excuse for leaving. (p. 232)

The hospital staff practice mutual pretense because they are in the business of curing patients.[32] Mutual pretense allows physicians seemingly to fulfill some of what is expected of them—to act as agents of our society's theodical project. "As long as they support the illusion that the children will get better, or at least can be made more comfortable," Bluebond-Langner comments, "they can carry out the procedures and duties that in part define them as physicians. . . . Further, by observing the seventh rule of mutual pretense, keeping the interactions brief, they can avoid becoming too involved" (pp. 218-19).[33]

----

32. Of course, this is not an intrinsic aim of medicine. For an argument that the role of medicine is to care, not to cure, see my book entitled *Suffering Presence: Theological Reflections on Medicine, the Mentally Handicapped, and the Church* (Notre Dame: University of Notre Dame Press, 1986).

33. Bluebond-Langner fails to indicate the powerful role of experimental medicine in the care of leukemic children. Certainly there is no question that our care, if not cure, of many of these children has

Given the obvious difficulties of mutual pretense, it might be assumed that a policy of "open awareness" would be preferable. However, only two children in Bluebond-Langner's study achieved open awareness, and she notes that it is far from clear that such awareness has good results. "The people who practiced open awareness," she points out, "did not accept the prognosis any more than those who practiced mutual pretense" (p. 221). Even more telling, "the practice of open awareness did not necessarily mean that the individuals felt any more comfortable around each other. The parents who practiced open awareness were as frequently absent from their children's room as parents who practiced mutual pretense" (pp. 221-22).

Open awareness caused other problems for hospital staff as well as parents, as Bluebond-Langner points out:

> The more one admits to children what is happening, the more there is to deal with, the greater the problems of 'acknowledging ultimate loss of the child and maintaining hope.' . . . This is seen most clearly in the terminal stages. How does one, after acknowledging the fact that the child will die, make the child go through with painful procedures,

---

improved dramatically in the dozen or so years since Bluebond-Langner did her research. But our medical response to leukemia has improved not because of any sudden breakthrough but because of the knowledge we have gained by performing this procedure on that child. Of course, in the process of acquiring this knowledge we have often used children for what are in effect medical experiments, even though we knew what we were doing could provide them with only minimal improvement. I have asked hematologists how they justified the use of these children in this manner as well as the unavoidability of playing on their parents' false hopes. They usually told me they simply tried not to think about it. We are now in the position of being able to help some leukemic children today because we treated others wrongly in the past.

especially where there is no guarantee that the relief will compensate for the pain of the procedure?

This is the conflict that the doctors and nurses felt most keenly. On one hand, how does one carry out painful procedures on children riddled with pain when there is not even a guarantee of relief? On the other hand, how does one stop procedures without feeling that all that went before (and that one is currently doing for others still in their first remission) was in vain? (pp. 227-28)

Bluebond-Langner notes that "this dilemma was not any more successfully resolved by staff members who practiced open awareness than by those who practiced mutual pretense" (p. 228).

In summary Bluebond-Langner emphasizes the children's extraordinary role in mutual pretense: "The onset of leukemia challenged the children's ability to meet the hopes of parents and society. They would not be able to become, to demonstrate their worth in future achievements, for they would have no future—that which defines one as being a child. The practice of mutual pretense allowed them to act as if they had a future, to act like children. By following the rules necessary for maintaining mutual pretense, they showed themselves responsive to the needs of others. The rewards for such behavior were great. They gained a sense of achievement, satisfaction, and worth in their own eyes and in the eyes of their caretakers. By reinforcing the adults' hopes, the children thereby guaranteed their continued presence. They were not left alone" (pp. 228-29).

Bluebond-Langner ends her book with no simple recommendations. She is not an advocate of open awareness, as if it were some magic technique that would make the pain go away. What she does recommend is a mixture of open awareness and mutual pretense that will allow the three groups involved—parents, children, and hospital staff—to continue their relationship with each other. She goes on to comment, "The children know both what their parents know and what they want to hear. They are more concerned with having parents around than with telling them the prognosis. Children will do whatever is necessary to keep their parents near [including maintaining pretenses about what they know], but they would often like to share their knowledge with someone else as well" (p. 235).

With the leukemic children Bluebond-Langner came to know, that "someone" often turned out to be Bluebond-Langner herself, because the children perceived her as outside of the system and learned to trust her. What advice does she give to the individual entrusted with that role?

> That person should listen to what the children say, taking cues from them, answering only what they ask, and on their terms. Remember, children will honor whatever rules are set up.
>
> The issue then is not whether to tell, but how to tell, in a way that respects the children and all of their many, often conflicting needs. (p. 235)

The larger problem, of course, is not whether we practice open awareness or mutual pretense, but what we have to say to our children about their death from leukemia and what we have to say about our death as "older children."[34]

---

34. During the entire time I was writing this book, and in particular while I was working on these last pages dealing with Bluebond-Langner's account, I thought very often of Elaine Scarry's treatment of pain in her book entitled *The Body in Pain: The Making and Unmaking*

Our inability to be with our children in their deaths, an inability that results in our children dying terribly alone, is but the result of our inability to deal with our own deaths. But our children's deaths bother us not only because they remind us of our own mortality, but also because they seem so pointless, because we believe that such children have not yet had the opportunity to "make a life," to develop a "life story." As a result, we often subject them to medical inter-

---

of the World (New York: Oxford University Press, 1985). The major theme of her book is the "unsharability" of pain—not only pain's unsharability but pain's power to destroy language. Pain, in effect, is the enemy of community precisely because we cannot feel one another's pain. Scarry's treatment of torture is so powerful because she documents the torturer's power to alienate us from our own experience—the torturer is literally able to destroy our world. (Scarry's analysis of torture cannot help but give even greater poignancy to *The Private Worlds of Dying Children*.) Scarry observes, however, that medicine is one of the ways we have of bringing pain into "the realm of public discourse": "For the success of the physician's work will often depend on the acuity with which he or she can hear the fragmentary language of pain, coax it into clarity, and interpret it" (p. 6). Yet Scarry also notes that the experience which many people have with the medical community "would bear out the opposite conclusion, the conclusion that physicians do not trust (hence, hear) the human voice, that they in effect perceive the voice of the patient as an 'unreliable narrator' of bodily events, a voice which must be bypassed as quickly as possible so that they can get around and behind it to the physical events themselves" (p. 6).

Of course, there are often good reasons for the physician's trying to "get around and behind" the patient's statement of pain "to the physical events themselves," but in the process the patient is only further alienated from his or her pain. Thus one of the great challenges facing modern medicine is how voice can be given to the patient's pain in a manner such that the therapy to relieve that pain does not further alienate the patient from his or her own experience. Needless to say, the problem becomes even more acute when dealing with children.

vention that has little or no point except the sustaining of life as an end in itself. We are just "buying time."

What we lack is the wisdom and skills of a community constituted by a truthful narrative that can comprehend such deaths without denying their pointlessness. In this respect it is revealing to note how Bluebond-Langner has structured her book. Rather than starting with the presentation of her "data," she begins with a chapter called "Children as Actors," in which she lays some groundwork, and in the next chapter presents a play entitled "The World of Jeffrey Andrews," which is based on the experiences of the children she met. Although the play (which makes up almost half the book) certainly is meant to exhibit her data—it contains many of the conversations she reports in support of her theory—I suspect that the play is the most truthful way she has to help us understand what she has learned by being with these children. Finally all she can do is tell a story.

Her play ends with a scene in which Jeffrey, who is now very close to death, asks her to read from *Charlotte's Web*. This is a wonderful story, of course, a story of friendship and loyalty. But what Jeffrey wants read to him is the last chapter, "where Charlotte dies." Jeffrey is right: this chapter contains a frank and realistic conversation about death. "'After all, what's a life, anyway?'" Charlotte says to Wilbur. "'We're born, we live a little while, we die. A spider's life can't help being something of a mess, after all this trapping and eating flies. By helping you perhaps I was trying to lift up my life a trifle. Heaven knows anyone's life can stand a little of that'" (pp. 129-30).

True, *Charlotte's Web* is also a story of hope. When Wilbur realizes that Charlotte is going to die, he decides that he can at least save her egg sac filled with little spiders.

Showing, for the first time, some genuine ingenuity, he gets Templeton, the rat, to rescue Charlotte's eggs by promising Templeton first chance at Wilbur's daily slop in the trough. Yet in the success of that adventure, we can forget how the story ends: "Next day, as the Ferris wheel was being taken apart and the race horses were being loaded into vans and the entertainers were packing up their belongings and driving away in their trailers, Charlotte died. The Fair Grounds were soon deserted. The sheds and buildings were empty and forlorn. The infield was littered with bottles and trash. Nobody, of the hundreds of people that had visited the Fair knew that a gray spider had played the most important part of all. No one was with her when she died" (p. 134). Shortly after Myra finishes the story, Jeffrey dies too.

But a child's death should not imitate a spider's. It may be that spiders are meant to live a little while and die, but we who are created for friendship with one another and with God cannot believe that this is "all there is." It may be that spiders are destined to die alone, but as those who believe that we are destined to enjoy one another and God, we cannot allow ourselves and our loved ones to so die. We have no theodicy that can soften the pain of our death and the death of our children, but we believe that we share a common story which makes it possible for us to be with one another especially as we die. There can be no way to remove the loneliness of the death of leukemic children unless they see witnessed in the lives of those who care for them a confidence rooted in friendship with God and with one another. That, finally, is the only response we have to "the problem" of the death of our children.

This book began with a quote from Nicholas Wolterstorff's book entitled *Lament for a Son*.[35] There Wolterstorff rightly notes that grief and suffering cannot help but isolate the sufferer. His book is an attempt to overcome that isolation by helping us share his suffering without offering any false or easy answers to explain why a twenty-five-year-old son might die in a climbing accident. Indeed, he rejects any attempt to give the death a meaning by fitting it into a pattern. Nor does he accept Rabbi Kushner's answer that God is also pained by death because God cannot do anything about it. Wolterstorff confesses, "I cannot fit it all together by saying, 'He did it,' but neither can I do so by saying, 'There was nothing he could do about it.' I cannot fit it together at all. I can only, with Job, endure. I do not know why God did not prevent Eric's death. To live without the answer is precarious. It's hard to keep one's footing" (p. 67).

Wolterstorff's pain does not make him question his faith, a faith nurtured by the same Dutch Calvinism that shaped Peter DeVries and Don Wanderhope. He expresses surprise that the elements of the gospel—particularly the hope of resurrection—he thought "would console did not." This does not make him believe any less in the resurrection. "Yet," he says, "Eric is gone, *here* and *now* he is gone; *now* I cannot talk with him, *now* I cannot see him, *now* I cannot hug him, *now* I cannot hear of his plans for the future. *That* is my sorrow. A friend said, 'Remember, he's in good hands.' I was deeply moved. But that reality does not put Eric back in my hands now. That's my grief. For that grief, what consolation can there be other than having him back?" (p. 31).

Wolterstorff acknowledges that "the Christian gospel

---

35. Wolterstorff, *Lament for a Son* (Grand Rapids: Eerdmans, 1987). All subsequent references will appear parenthetically in the text.

tells us more of the meaning of sin than of suffering. . . . To the 'why' of suffering we get no firm answer. Of course some suffering is easily seen to be the result of our sin: war, assault, poverty amidst plenty, the hurtful word. And maybe some is chastisement. But not all. The meaning of the remainder is not told us. It eludes us. Our net of meaning is too small. There's more to our suffering than our guilt" (p. 74).

Like God, we suffer because we love, so we must acknowledge what Wolterstorff does:

> Suffering is down at the center of things, deep down where the meaning is. Suffering is the meaning of our world. For Love is the meaning. And Love suffers. The tears of God are the meaning of history.
>
> But mystery remains. Why isn't Love-*without*-suffering the meaning of things? Why is *suffering*-Love the meaning? Why does God endure his suffering? Why does he not at once relieve his agony by relieving ours? (p. 90)

Wolterstorff is wise enough not to try to answer these perhaps misshapen questions. To do so would betray his helplessness, which he discusses with painful wisdom: "I know now about helplessness—of what to do when there is nothing to do. I have learned coping. We live in a time and place where, over and over, when confronted with something unpleasant we pursue not coping but overcoming. Often we succeed. Most of humanity has not enjoyed and does not enjoy such luxury. Death shatters our illusion that we can make do without coping. When we have overcome absence with phone calls, winglessness with airplanes, summer heat with air-conditioning—when we have overcome all these and much more besides, then there will abide two things with which we must cope: the evil in our hearts and death. There are those who vainly think that some technology will even enable us to overcome the former. Everyone knows that there is no technology for overcoming death. Death is left for God's overcoming" (pp. 72-73).

Just as Wolterstorff is not interested in false or easy answers, so he is not interested in false or easy comfort. So do not tell Wolterstorff that death—the death of Eric—is "not really so bad. Because it is. Death is awful, demonic. If you think your task as comforter is to tell me that really, all things considered, it's not so bad, you do not sit with me in my grief but place yourself off in the distance away from me. Over there, you are of no help. What I need to hear from you is that you recognize how painful it is. I need to hear from you that you are with me in my desperation. To comfort me, you have to come close. Come sit beside me on my mourning bench" (p. 34).

The author and publisher gratefully acknowledge permission to quote material from the following publications:

Excerpts from *The Blood of the Lamb* by Peter DeVries. Copyright © 1961 by Peter DeVries. Reprinted with permission of Little, Brown & Company.

Excerpts from *God and Human Suffering: An Exercise in the Theology of the Cross* by Douglas John Hall. Copyright © 1986 by Augsburg Publishing House. Reprinted with permission of Augsburg Fortress Publishers.

Excerpts from *The Message of the Psalms* by Walter Brueggemann. Copyright © 1984 by Augsburg Publishing House. Reprinted with permission of Augsburg Fortress Publishers.

Excerpts from *The Private Worlds of Dying Children* by Myra Bluebond-Langner. Copyright © 1978 by Princeton University Press. Reprinted with permission of Princeton University Press.

Excerpts from *Setting Limits: Medical Goals in an Aging Society* by Daniel Callahan. Copyright © 1987 by Daniel Callahan. Reprinted with permission of Simon & Schuster.

Excerpts from *Theology and the Problem of Evil* by Kenneth Surin. Copyright © 1986 by Basil Blackwell. Reprinted with permission of Basil Blackwell.

Excerpts from *Where Is God When a Child Suffers?* by Penny Giesbrecht. Copyright © 1988 by Hannibal Books. Reprinted with permission of Hannibal Books, 921 Center St., Hannibal, Mo. 63401.

Index

Index